if i Had Three Wishes,
the Only ONE would Be...

if i Had Three Wishes, the Only ONE Would Be...

Your Personalized Plan
for Discovering Your Life Goals,
Igniting Your Spirit Power,
and Making Your Dreams Come Alive

Joyce Chapman, M.A.

Newcastle Publishing
North Hollywood, California

Copyright 1995 by Joyce Chapman. Published by Newcastle Publishing Company, Inc., P.O. Box 7589, Van Nuys, California 91409. All rights reserved. No part of this book may be reproduced in any form without the express written consent of the publisher, except by a reviewer, who may quote brief passages in connection with a review.

Edited by Gina Gross Misiroglu
Cover and interior design © 1995 Michele Lanci-Altomare
Interior diagrams by Amy Inouye
Cover illustration © 1995 Sheri Matlack

ISBN: 0-87877-199-9
A Newcastle Book
First printing 1995
10 9 8 7 6 5 4 3 2 1
Printed in the United States of America.

My dream is to lift the world above those who would destroy it through environmental, political, and spiritual neglect. To accomplish this, I work with those people willing to improve tomorrow's world by making changes in themselves today. This book is dedicated to those eager to realize their dreams, for the future of our world requires individual fulfillment of each of our highest and noblest aspirations.

—Joyce Chapman

CONTENTS

INTRODUCTION—1

CHAPTER 1
Opening the Door to a New Dream—15

CHAPTER 2
Breaking Free of Old Mindsets—45

CHAPTER 3
Living from Your Fullest Spirit Power—73

CHAPTER 4
Crossing the Threshold—113

CHAPTER 5
Living Your Dream in the Real World—139

CHAPTER 6
Celebrating Your Dream—167

ACKNOWLEDGMENTS

I wish to acknowledge all those dreamers who took the last page of my first book, *Live Your Dream*, seriously enough to insist upon dreaming even higher. The steps to doing that is what this book provides, thanks to publisher Al Saunders and his belief in this work. Thanks, too, to Diane Chalfant who helped formulate the first draft; Eldonna Laye, whom I call my "spirit writer" and with whom I shared joy through taking ideas higher . . . and higher; Gina Misiroglu for her dedication to excellence in editing; to artists Michele Lanci-Altomare and Sheri Matlack for capturing the essence of the book; to all those who participated in workshops and surveys; to those whose stories illustrate different methods of living their dreams; and to the members of my family—all of whom are busily living quite wonderful dreams of their own.

If I Had Three Wishes,
the Only ONE Would Be . . .

INTRODUCTION

The idea for a book dedicated to achieving one's ultimate life's purpose did not come to me overnight. Although I'd like to take sole credit for having concocted the premise for this book in my sleep, the truth of the matter is that it was developed over several years, through a number of "life lessons," mainly those of my clients, workshop participants, family, and myself. Although I laid the groundwork for reaching your ultimate dream in my first books, time and time again sensitive souls came to me and told me of their experiences, and of their lack of and need for an advanced road map, or set of constructive life tools, for taking what they had learned and, in essence, applying it to something greater. Although many people had successfully completed their dreamwork and felt that they were indeed living their dream, there was a real yearning for something *more*. In many cases, people had simply redefined their dream, or life's course of events had naturally advanced them to another plane of living. Sometimes life just simply deals you another—unexpected—hand. I felt there needed to be a guide for those people who wanted to live their ultimate life's purpose. This book is my answer to that basic human trait of simply wanting to be everything that you can be.

This is an *advanced* course, written for those who have completed the work required to become highly evolved students of consciousness. A structured series of exercises to begin, then maintain, upper levels of self-realization were provided in my first books, *Live Your Dream, Journaling for Joy*, and their related workbooks. Through them, you have learned that writing your way to personal growth and freedom is a lifelong process.

With this self-examination greater and greater truths are revealed. With these truths you have accomplished earlier dreams. Now that you are ready to move on to bigger—and higher—dreams, you are ready to dedicate yourself to reaching your fullest potential. Having already chosen values, beliefs, and habits that are consistent with earlier dreams, you have found the joy in learning each of your life's experiences. Having worked with my or comparable self-help works, you have come to recognize the differences between vision and delusion, between faulty thinking, fantasy, and reality. You also know that being exposed to new ideas alone is never enough; you must acknowledge, prepare for, and work toward dreams if they are to be achieved.

This book, and its companion workbook, provide the series of steps you will need to discover, liberate, then celebrate any known or latent dream(s). Activities and assignments show you how to focus your energy to clarify your quest and help you understand that the fulfillment of your dream is important to more than just you, for only when enough of us align with, and activate, our personal dreams will we have a better world.

So, I applaud your readiness for this next step. I cheer your eagerness to reach your individual best. I congratulate you on your decision to accept even more of your own personal power. I rejoice in your dedication to fulfilling your destiny, and I look forward to celebrating with you as you complete each exercise in this book and take each step in the companion workbook. I suggest that you also purchase a large art pad—to provide a large enough "canvas" for your dream. And, as always, keep close at hand a wide selection of colored pens for those activities requiring them. Exercises for you to engage in are set apart from the body of the text in italicized type.

Get ready, right now, to join with others who are stepping over the boundaries of small and ordinary thinking into higher levels of thought—that kind of innovative contemplation resulting in the design of new structures instead of patching together those that don't work anymore. The kind of thinking that creates a new environment that nourishes our spirits instead of denying, or depleting, them. The format for turning your primary wish into an attainable dream requires clarity and focus so—let us begin the process necessary to liberate and claim your highest dream.

The following pages of guidelines serve as your road map. They are outlined here in the introduction for quick reference, but, more importantly, the book is built around these simple concepts, so that you can structure the way you approach your dream in a way that the book is structured. In other words, if you were to hold your dream up to a mirror, it would reflect back this simple process of taking your dream from concept to reality. This textbook for your "dream coursework" has a simple format: the book explores these themes, one by one, provides examples of real-life people who have followed them, and suggests ways that you might implement them into your personal agenda of fulfilling your dream. You might find that you refer back to this handy synopsis every so often for an overview of the path you will walk while realizing your dream.

Liberating Your Dream

You may, or may not, know what your ultimate dream is, so ask yourself the following questions: Do you find yourself hampered by the role you are playing? Too often, we get caught up in job descriptions and roles, rather than in our missions. Have you been so busy being a good dad, mom, son, daughter, boss, or employee that you've suppressed or put aside what you *really* want to do? Or perhaps you've dismissed an earlier dream as adolescent, or even presumptuous. After all, how can a single person feed the world, make the planet safe for all children, establish world peace, or write an inspirational book? Have you abandoned an earlier dream because you lack the necessary credentials, or the money, or the time?

Well, like all your earlier journeys, this one begins with a single step. So, begin the same way you began in *Live Your Dream*: by re-examining yourself by doing the prescribed exercises. By the end of this introduction, you may know exactly what your next dream is. If so, this is a wonderful place to start. You may only have a glimmer. If so, this is a wonderful place to start! Or, you may still be blocked. If so, this, too, is a wonderful place to begin. What is important is that you claim whatever you perceive your dream—however fragmentary—to be at this moment.

The next step is moving forward with it. By doing so, you begin to step even more fully into your own personal power, and ways of assuming even more responsibility for that power. Next, you'll learn ways of truthfully explaining to others what you are about to do, or become. Following that, you will learn ways in which to evaluate your progress. And, from there, you will master ways in which to move beyond life's obstructions to become what I call a dream activator.

Getting Rid of Old Mindsets

No matter how successful we've been so far, we still carry within us old ideas and opinions that may no longer serve us. Indeed, those very convictions may be what will keep us from manifesting what we want most in the world. The most difficult part of identifying which beliefs are most restrictive is that we've never questioned them before. Now is the time for you to do precisely that—so that your dream can become a reality.

The Never Again . . . portions of the chapters are designed so that you can address the specific issues that each particular chapter covers. These parts of the chapters allow you to take a close look at what's been holding you back, and allow you the freedom to write about them intimately. Upon close examination, you'll probably discover that your old mindsets are so limiting, so power-draining, they serve no purpose to fulfilling your dream. Allow yourself the time to acknowledge that these mindsets exist, then blow them into the air, symbolizing a new beginning that has no room for limiting beliefs.

Claiming Your Biggest Dream

The bigger the dream, the bigger the impact. In fact, your *ultimate* dream may be far bigger than you yet realize. But, admit as much of the dream as you know right now. By acknowledging the pieces of the dream puzzle that you know, you begin the process of fulfilling your purpose. Just remember to be aware of additional parts of your puzzle as they emerge because, if what you really want to do is make America safe for children, you don't want to limit yourself to opening a local day-care center.

So, for any of you who have consciously put an old dream on hold, think about those elderly adults who voice regrets for opportunities lost, or hopes unfilled. It was perhaps best said by John Greenleaf Whittier in his poem, "Maud Muller":

> For of all sad words of tongue or pen
> The saddest are these: "it might have been."

If you once dreamed of becoming a writer, an actor, or a doll maker, review that dream again. Then, don't allow yourself to be deterred by anything, especially immediate personal needs. Remember, there is *always* enough time and money to pursue a dream. Like magnets, time and money contributing to the well-being of the planet attract additional time and money—maybe not as quickly as we'd like, but they do manifest; if only in the nick of time. The question to ask yourself if time or money is not arriving in a timely manner is—*Is my dream high enough?* And, if you are in doubt . . . *Take it higher!* So, if you want to develop a more perfect engine or a cure for common diseases and find yourself running into block walls at every turn, *re-evaluate* what you are doing, and how you are doing it. Is your dream big enough? High enough? What *other* methods might be explored? When your dream is high enough, help and helpers are waiting to be found. Just open your mind to the infinite number of options and people available to you. Then go after them!

The Make the Dream Real . . . Make It Yours portions of the chapters exist to help you claim your biggest dream. After finishing reading the book chapters, these sections allow you to, in essence, write your own chapter; that is, to really write about what your dream means to you at that point in your journey. Through this journaling, you validate your dream and chronicle the necessary pieces of your dream in order to more fully ingrain it in your personality, your daily walk in life, and the world.

Accepting and Releasing Your Personal and Spiritual Powers

By accepting the responsibility of your idea, you begin using even more of your own inner powers. Even though you have already experienced the immense growth that comes with acknowledging and using personal power, the concept of using spiritual power may make you uneasy. That's because the abuses and misuses of power are all around us. But I am not talking about power that uses or controls others. That kind of power, driven by anger, insecurity, or fear, arises when people use ego to accomplish their ends rather than spirit. Operating at the level of the ego, we seek to control, dominate, and manipulate to make others do our will. While that may accomplish our ends for a time, it never lasts because no one feels safe around us. Working at the level of spirit, however, allows us to show others *by our example* that being creative, loving, intuitive, joyful, expressive, effective, responsible, independent, direct, dynamic, energetic, free, and true to who you really are stands to benefit them as well as you. Another way of explaining this most vital component of personal empowerment is that when we live in our spirit power, we energize those around us. And by energizing them, we are showing them how to become more of who they are. So, use your powers by passing them on!

Think about the aforementioned concepts and labels until you fully understand the difference between personal, spirit, and ego power because the power I speak of, grounded as it is in love, is never driven by anger or insecurity. Instead, it is part and parcel of the loftiest levels of the human spirit. As such, it is refueled by the never-ending supply of energy available to us when we access our inner power and become one with the collective unconscious. In other words, the higher you elevate your thinking, the higher you raise your awareness; the more developed you become, the more you improve the world around you. The power to transform oneself is *the real* power that you seek.

As you have already discovered, once you have accepted and assimilated your power, you find yourself living in the same world but seeing it from an entirely new position. While old problems may tag along, your newfound view allows you to put what you perceived as adversity into fresh perspective. Problems, then, are no longer seen as punishment, but as ways of continuing your personal growth. A fresh perspective may be needed even as you are reading this paragraph. Just as I remind my clients, "You have the ability to leave this moment totally different from when you arrived." It is true for you, too. You don't have to finish reading this paragraph with the same beliefs you held when you began. Right now, you can make the decision to become *fully* empowered, to move beyond a comfortable status quo, to gain even more control over the direction of your life. So if you have been reluctant to assume more of your personal power, think about it again!

Assuming Total Responsibility

How many people have you known who have confessed to having a terrific idea, only to abandon it when it began demanding commitment, change, hard work, support from friends and family, or money? Put another way, how many dreams have *you* not yet put into action?

Granted, it's not always easy to remain enthusiastic when friends, colleagues, and family members doubt your capabilities or ideas. And, a blinding flash of creativity seems less magical when years of research and certification lay ahead. Patents, lawyers, lessons, schooling, and business travel take time and money—commodities that often appear to be unavailable. Yet it is in accepting that those things are unavailable that separates the dream activator from the everyday dreamer. The people I call dream activators *do whatever needs to be done to make their dream come true!* Dreamers often just fantasize about what would happen if their dream came true. Without taking action, a dreamer may continue to fantasize.

Fearful of making a fool of yourself? Afraid of committing yourself to a course of action that might fail? Cautious of making uncomfortable financial moves? Of course—it would be irresponsible not to consider all of these things. Yet, you can't allow yourself to be immobilized by cautions that hide your dream in the shadow of your psyche. Lost dreams don't do anything for anyone. Your commitment to yourself requires that you assume total responsibility for your own progress. And there is another commitment involved, too. I dedicated this book to "those eager to realize their dreams, for the future of our world requires individual fulfillment of each of our highest and noblest aspirations." So, whenever you put day-to-day needs ahead of your dream, you are denying the world your measure of fulfillment. Remember that whenever bills become overwhelming, or a forward step appears too fraught with chance. Then, remind yourself to pay attention to your *inner* needs. Acting upon what you discover, begin behaving as if you are already living the life you want so dearly. The world you save will be your own.

Telling Your Own Truth to Empower Your Dream

Find your truth. You can't hide behind lies, deception, or fluff. Nor can you take the easy way out, telling others what you think they want to hear, or what you think is acceptable or achievable. It may take some serious digging to discover your primary truth.

To see, hear, and align with that truth, you must be willing to feel everything, think everything, and express everything. Let go of the fear. Don't hold back. Talk your way into realizing your biggest dream. When you talk about your biggest dream, censorship just gets in the way. We've all been trained to be considerate, to protect others from a direct experience of our unedited opinions. But your dream is not a danger to anyone else. To the contrary, living your dream frees those around you to live their own. Only when we come right out and say what we're thinking do we create an environment for change.

Forming Your Own Empowerment Team

Even if you have not fully identified your dream, you probably know the direction in which you want to go. So, whatever field you wish to be in, get yourself appropriately trained or educated and start associating with those already there! Association provides contacts and friendships that allow you to practice living in your dream. As you move forward, affiliate yourself with people who will be traveling with you. Members of your team may include family members and old friends, mentors, advisors, and coaches.

Practicing Standing Aside

Stepping back from situations allows you to make unemotional observations, inferences, and decisions. Detach yourself from what others are doing or saying. I know what you are thinking—and you are right—it is a paradox to care with all your heart and soul about something, then be asked to give up controlling the path! How does one practice being detached when feeling so passionately? By tapping into the universe and making decisions from your inner self. Live in the state of "Oh!" by letting go of preconceived notions of how things should be—or how they should be accomplished. Then step back and examine everything that you are doing or thinking that isn't really you. If, for instance, you still need someone else to approve or give you permission, you have not yet accepted responsibility for your own power.

If your spouse, or friends, or parents aren't supportive, find companions who do believe in you—and don't expose your ideas and plans to those who ridicule or doubt them. While it would be wonderful to have those closest to you on your empowerment team, it would be unusual! So enjoy relatives and friends for who and what they are. Just don't demand, or even expect, them to align with you.

Getting through the Tough Times

Situations and events are bound to happen when you are moving forward. When they do, reach out for assistance when you need it. Depending upon the kind of block you encounter, choose the type of coaching/advice/expertise that will move you beyond the impediment. That may be professional guidance, it may be a friend, or it may be time alone. It is important that you do what you need to do to learn from what is impeding your progress, then move beyond— or around—it.

The most common stumbling block that adults accept is that they don't have enough money to accomplish their dreams. If you buy into that, you will not only never achieve your dreams—you won't even perceive them! Don't take my word for it, just take a moment to observe the world's natural abundance. You may not have tapped into as much of it as you'd like yet, but there is more than enough food and water and shelter for you and everyone else on the planet. It is just the *distribution* of this largesse that is limited. So don't allow this notion or lack of resources limit you!

Notifying Yourself and Others if Your Focus Changes

We've all lived out a life choice that turned out to be incongruent with who we thought we were . . . or could be. For that reason, I can't overemphasize the importance of being open to changing your focus or direction when needed. What is vital is admitting to yourself that you are changing direction—even if at first glance the alteration appears to indicate indecisiveness, or lack of direction. Most other great dreamers adapted their plans, timelines, or goals. Don't fear this! And don't regard it as some sort of failure, because it's growth in action. My way of handling this situation is to live from one of my favorite phrases: It's up to me to know what I want, and it's up to my spirit to figure out how!

Living Congruently with Your Dream, Self, Place, Possessions, and Position

By doing the aforementioned, you begin moving into the inner realm of consciousness. Rejoice by *establishing a schedule that makes the realization of your dream a top priority*. That includes allowing time for inspirational thought and creative action. Set aside time to be with those who nurture and empower you. And at the beginning and end of each day, lift your face skyward to embrace what is, and what will be. For change, however unsteady, is essential— reminding you that you are alive and *growing*. So *practice* those changes that allow you to live congruently with your dream.

Celebrating Your Dream

It's your natural right to make your own life choices. By claiming the dream you've chosen—by setting up your schedule to make your dream your top priority—you free your energy to do what you've always wanted to do. From then on you work at the jobs you really love, associate with people you really want to be around. Simply by embracing change you begin to grow. So, welcome changes and start celebrating right now. Just by reading this introduction you have probably learned something about yourself that you did not know before you began.

By reading this far, you have opened yourself to a host of new ideas. This should lead you to ask yourself, Where am I in my wishes, hopes, and dreams process right now? and What do I intend to gain from reading this book?

Take a few days to ponder these questions, and record your responses on the blank pages that follow. You may discover (or really start to *own*) some very interesting facets of yourself and your life.

CHAPTER 1

Opening the Door to a New Dream

IF YOU'VE READ MY OTHER BOOKS, YOU KNOW THE IMPORTANCE I place on dreaming dreams and achieving their fulfillment. So, what old dreams are you celebrating right now? Celebration is the human way of savoring well-earned rewards. As a veteran dreamer, you have flown in the face of "hard, scientific evidence" by making earlier wishes come true. Wasn't success wonderful? And isn't it equally thrilling to know that it was through your own efforts that those dreams were manifested? Now, having become used to using your talents, gifts, and options, you can look back and see how much you influenced—perhaps even redefined—your own personal future.

But there is much, much more to you than you can even imagine. Let's get in touch with that by looking ahead at your future and factoring into it all of your current wishes, hopes, and dreams. Pretend . . . just pretend . . . that you have been given ten wishes. What would they be?

Settle back into your favorite dreaming position. Take out your favorite pen and your journal and make a list of the top ten things you want to add to your life. Now, using colored pens, fully illustrate each of the ten. Having done that, slowly and thoughtfully contemplate your wishes—enjoy them. Then put the list where it will not be disturbed. Think about them often over the next few days. Hold them in your heart. Allow those wishes to germinate in your mind, for this is the way to liberate your one dream . . . and make it real.

For a perfect example of releasing a dream, you need to look no farther than Linda, a New York publishing house editor who was always cognizant of her wishes, hopes, and dreams.

Having spent years rising to the top of her profession, at thirty-three, Linda assessed what she had accomplished and was pleased. But, there were things about living and working in New York that were less than perfect. And, in working for one company, she was restricted in the types of manuscripts she was given. On top of that, in working so hard to establish herself, she had chosen to delay marriage and a family . . . and biologically . . . time was running out. So Linda set out to redesign her life.

Her new design called for a new job; one providing her with the time to include being a wife and mother. With an outstanding reputation established in New York, she decided to chance moving to California, where she set herself up as a free-lance editor. Next on her list of "to dos" was finding a wonderful husband and, eventually, having a baby. Today, five years later, she has all those things. And her free-lance editing business is thriving.

Liberating Your Newest Dream

How wonderful to already have a good understanding of who and what you are. Now it is time to open the door wide on who you are, what you wish, and what you can achieve! As someone who has completed earlier dreams, you no longer find it frightening to accept your own responsibility for your personal mental, physical, and spiritual growth. Yet, having accomplished that growth, you may still feel a yearning to know even more about yourself, sensing that there is something else within waiting to be released. For those with the urge to find out, not knowing strikes at your soul! If you were born to dance and have not yet embraced the performer inside, a vital part of you remains waiting in the shadows. So it is time to unveil what may lay slumbering inside.

As you have learned, in the process of making any dream come true, you attract like-minded people with whom to share your ideas and goals. That process has drawn us together because my dream is to coach those willing to seek their destinies. So, right now, take time to clear your mind because, despite all the work you've done to rid yourself of earlier limitations and beliefs, you still carry your history with you. Some of those memories may be holding you back from moving forward.

Mentally fill a chalkboard with a list of everything standing in the way of your forward motion. Review it. Now, erase that list and begin to prepare yourself for the changes that are to come—for the world depends upon the achievement of your dreams.

As an ancient Chinese proverb promises:

> If there is righteousness in the heart,
> There will be beauty in the character.
> If there is beauty in the character,
> There will be harmony in the home.
> If there is harmony in the home,
> There will be order in the nation.
> When there is order in the nation,
> There will be peace in the world.

In other words, we must not underestimate the importance of the individual—you or me or anyone else. If there is ever to be worldwide peace, it must begin within each one of us. And as we change in our view of the world, and ourselves, so do those around us. Only when we are pleased with our own progress do we freely encourage others to work toward their own fulfillment. You found this to be true while working toward earlier dreams— your family, friends, and colleagues responded to the changes you made. Yet, here you are again, suspecting there is another—perhaps even *higher* dream— that will make more differences in your life and theirs! Again, maybe you have only *sensed* that dream, intuitively felt it buried deep and unidentified within

Opening the Door to a New Dream

you. Or, perhaps you have glimpsed portions of it, but have not been able to put them all together. Dreams are often like unassembled puzzles, and you suspect that yours is just waiting for you to put its missing sections together. Simply by embracing that process, you continue the journey toward discovery and accomplishment.

What's missing from your wish list? Do you have anything you wish to add? Combine? Delete? Alter? Do that!

Consciousness as Unexplored Territory

The traveling salesman in *The Music Man* said, "You gotta know the territory!" and he was right! Identifying a secret dream is a journey into unknown territory because the process of finding it calls for you to consciously send your thoughts forward into uncharted terrain. Trailblazing physician Deepak Chopra states that "consciousness is a force that most of us undervalue. Generally," he says, "we do not focus our inner awareness or use its real power, even in the most difficult moments of crisis." Even less do we value our *unconscious* mind—that personal pool of intelligence and instinct that comes from a combination of the knowledge contained in our genes and life experiences. With all of the recent scientific discoveries on DNA, heredity, and genetic programming, why do we continue to underrate our potential? I believe we deny our power because acknowledging something of value requires that we accept personal responsibility for it. Rather than be held accountable for the failure or success of our ambitions and dreams, we all too often deny our ability to deliberately manifest what we want. It is, after all, much easier to blame bad luck or others for not having or becoming. To use more of our own powerful consciousness, we must access our unconscious by trusting our instincts—and our wishes and dreams. And we strengthen both through meditation, prayer, dream interpretation, journal writing, and therapy. We can then access even more energies and knowledge beyond our own genetic and experiential make-up.

This is not totally new territory. Throughout the ages, creative people have tapped into the power of what psychologist Carl Jung called the "collective unconscious"—I visualize the collective unconscious as an ultimate library containing all of what we already know in the universe, and what is yet to be discovered. To reach the collective unconscious' highest potential, Jung said that "we must each find our own." It's a closed loop, you see; to reach ultimate knowledge, we must first develop ourselves to our fullest potential! So, before we can align ourselves with this state of consciousness, we must reaffirm the power and importance of our own conscious and unconscious thoughts. Each of us, then, is an integral part of life on this planet. Therefore, it is imperative that we develop our individual talents and abilities to the fullest so that we will be ready when our highest dreams are revealed. Make no mistake about it—everyone else in the world depends upon you reaching your dream if harmony is to be achieved!

Does that mean that your dream must immediately and conspicuously benefit the rest of humanity? A Hebrew saying has it, "He who saves a single soul, saves the world entire!" Was it Oskar Schindler's original intent to save 1,100 Jews from death during World War II? Certainly not—he wanted to make money. Lots of it! In the process of striving for his initial dream—which would only have benefited himself— he discovered a larger one. Along with it, he discovered inner strength and integrity that few had suspected. And so, he has gone down in history as the man who saved over a thousand Jews from certain death. Today, eleven thousand descendants of those saved are alive because Schindler's original dream grew. So, however large your dream seems to you, it is probably bigger. Say you are dreaming of creating a loving home for your family, or of inventing a more effective filing system for your office. These dreams may not immediately make life better for your neighbors, or for office workers across town. Yet, every improvement in the world eventually benefits others. Did Henry Ford have any idea of the extent of the change he would initiate by instituting mass production of automobiles? Probably not—but in one way or another he changed the lives of every human being on this planet! So, when you align yourself with the limitlessness of the universe, you will not only realize your own dream but, eventually, you will improve life for people you will never know. So, it is now time to write your story . . . the story of *your* dream!

Opening the Door to a New Dream

Giving yourself plenty of peace, quiet, time, a journal or notebook, and a favorite pen, begin recording everything you remember about your last dream. Then, using the aforementioned people as models, include a list of everyone who was affected by your dream as you were working toward it. Add those who were affected when your dream was realized.

By looking back at how you achieved your last dream, you have opened the door to your next one.

Now, think about what you are wishing, hoping, and dreaming. Take out your pen and paper again and write about what's beyond the door. Let's play "Let's pretend" to reveal what you are seeing—and what you want to see!

To actually move beyond the door, you must be able to feel, taste, smell, and envision your dream. You've done this before so, closing your eyes, make a wish. After all, wishes and hopes are the stuff that dreams are made of. The following exercise helps you start to pull all the pieces of your dream together.

Take ten minutes to clear your mind, to reopen the door to a new dream. Take ten to gain insight, understanding, and clarity. To free yourself. To lift your spirits. To identify a block. To step into your power. To find an answer, although it doesn't need to be written in stone yet. Take ten minutes to invite yourself to be back in the celebration of your creative spirit.

The following writing prompts are designed to help you take exactly ten minutes to get your life "on purpose." They may be used in several ways:

★ *Close your eyes, run your fingers down the page, stop, and prepare to write using the prompt your finger lands on.*

★ *Playfully let your glance fall on any one of the prompts, and write about it.*

★ *Consciously select a prompt that appeal to you, or a prompt that will provide information for an issue you are dealing with, and write about it.*

★ *Go down the lists, reviewing each question at a time, and answer all of them.*

Whatever method you prefer for making your selection, choose a prompt and write it at the top of a blank page, set a timer for exactly ten minutes, and write using the following sequence of questions:

- ★ *What is my initial, uncensored thought? (three minutes)*

- ★ *What's holding me back? (one minute, maximum)*

- ★ *What insight would bring me to acknowledging my biggest dream? (three minutes)*

- ★ *After rereading what I've written, what is my specific plan for action? What will I do, and when will I have it done by? What do I need to write more about? (three minutes)*

The realization of a dream can only be developed within one's innermost being. The purpose behind using these prompts as idea starters is to lead yourself fully into trusting yourself, fully motivating yourself, fully recognizing yourself, and bringing your dreams into reality. For many people, this is the hardest step: Once you get to the place of knowing what you need to know, are you willing to *live* it?

Welcome to the promtings that may very well change your life. . . .

- ＊ Am I a dreamer?

- ＊ What was I born to do?

- ＊ What am I here to do?

- ＊ What am I doing to fulfill my destiny?

- ＊ What am I doing, being, and having that's helping me to live in the excitement of realizing my biggest dream?

- ＊ Is my dream the "right" dream?

- ＊ What will I have to do every moment of every day, once my dream is started in motion?

- ＊ How will I plan a schedule for my dream?

- ＊ What natural abilities do I have that allow for the development of my dreams?

- ＊ What skills do I have in place that free me to live my dream?

* What do I know about dreamers who have decided to live and celebrate their biggest dreams?

* What have life's experiences taught me?

* What rumors do I want to hear about myself celebrating my biggest dream?

* The biggest dream I have realized to date is _____.

* How did I celebrate the realization of my biggest dream to date?

* The claiming of my biggest dream has awakened me to the following smaller dreams. . . .

* What are the stages of my dreamer self?

* What belief statements empower me?

* In what situations do I take risks? In what situations do I hesitate to take risks?

* What do I have to do to become an actualized dreamer?

* What do I need to go beyond to become an actualized dreamer?

* What path is mine to choose?

* Am I having fun yet?

* Whom do I need to surround myself with so that my dream is possible?

* Is the work I now engage in bringing me the money I need and want?

* Am I practicing what would allow me to have my biggest impact on the world?

* What did I do today to prevent myself from living my dream?

* What happened in my life yesterday that taught me something?

* What am I doing today to apply the lessons I learned from yesterday?

* Is realizing my dream worth changing for?

* What do I want and need to value today, this week, this month, this year?

✳ What stretch do I need to turn my dream into a reality?

✳ Am I taking full responsibility for the realization of my dream?

✳ If I had just arrived on the planet and my job was to teach others to dream, what would I teach them? What would my plan be?

✳ In what ways can I contribute to the lives of others?

✳ What did I do, or can I do, to enhance and enrich someone's life today?

✳ What should definitely be on my schedule today?

✳ What am I going to need on my journey? Expand upon the idea of taking the right road with the right wardrobe, supplies packed, road map in hand.

✳ Do I want to reclaim any of my shattered dreams, or claim any left by the wayside?

✳ Who am I?

✳ What stories have I collected on my way to realizing my big dream? Make a list of story titles. Choose one of these stories to write, and then share it with someone.

✳ What are the stages of my claiming my power?

✳ Here are fifty ways I celebrate my power.

✳ Have I lost my power?

✳ Do I have a spirit of liberation?

✳ Am I feeling powerful?

✳ Am I looking powerful?

✳ What needs to be released in order for me to step into my power?

✳ What secrets am I keeping from myself?

✳ Is it hard work to realize my potential?

✳ Am I willing to do the work necessary to realize my potential?

✳ Write ten affirmations that empower you to embark upon your biggest dream.

✳ Write twenty-five beliefs that will empower you.

Opening the Door to a New Dream

- ✳ Write a letter to someone from your past and tell him or her what your biggest dream is. Convince the person that you have no doubt you will succeed.
- ✳ List ways to make your dream known.
- ✳ Write your job description.
- ✳ Make a list of outrageous accomplishments you already achieved.
- ✳ Make a list of shattered dreams.
- ✳ Make a list of unclaimed dreams.
- ✳ List the ways in which stepping into your dream empowers you.
- ✳ What's next?

Never Again...

Never again do you need to resist or doubt your learning!

Now that you've completed these dream pages, you'll never again have to be afraid to open the door to any new dream. By integrating the learning from this first chapter, you've given yourself permission to be successful. Right here—right now—address these issues to reaffirm your willingness to embrace your fulfilled dream. As you work through the Never Again section of each chapter, you are putting old ways behind you and claiming the new.

In your everyday life, write about what you've read that helped you open your door.

Opening the Door to a New Dream

List statements you've overheard that helped empower you to keep that door open.

List the radio and television programs that helped develop your sense of self.

List the films that have reminded you that you are able to attain any dream.

Write about the real and fictional people who have influenced you to strive to reach your destiny. Define in tangible terms what these people have "given" you, whether they be character traits, words of wisdom, or objects.

Reveal some personal revelations that might need investigating.

Now, you are better able to accept the responsibility of making your dream a reality. It will be most valuable for you to continue doing this in a highly visual way. As Shakespeare wrote, "All the world is a stage," and you are now coming up out of the audience to take your rightful place on a stage of your own making. In later chapters, you will be writing the script that you want to follow.

For right now, however, draw in the space below those things that you want in your life—starting right now.

Opening the Door to a New Dream

Whatever you see you can incorporate into your life. In the introduction, twelve basic guidelines were introduced to direct you toward fulfillment. Addressing each will let you know if you are ready and willing to make the changes today that will make your dream possible tomorrow.

While you may, or may not, know what your ultimate dream is, you now understand that, like all journeys, this one begins with a single step. By re-examining yourself, you have discovered much that you did know, and maybe more that you were not consciously aware of. From this you have grown in your perception of yourself. You also understand the importance of never underestimating the role you play in the universal scheme of things. Then, too, you have identified some of the things that have stood in the way of opening the door to your dream. So, even if your dream is not fully identified, now is time to start moving forward.

Write about what all this means to you.

Opening the Door to a New Dream

Do you yet understand your dream—your destiny?

Are you willing to do the work required to realize your potential?

Are you willing to make necessary changes in yourself?

What changes are you willing to make?

Write about what other changes need be made to make your dream come true.

Discuss what you have to do to set the liberation of your dream in motion.

Are you willing to make each of those changes?

Make the Dream Real ... Make It Yours

To instill the reality of your dream in your subconscious as well as your conscious mind, address the following issues even though they may appear repetitious. Writing your thoughts and feelings down in different forms makes them more real. It also allows you to carry them with you, so on the following pages write your declarations. After you've completed the following pages, you may want to photocopy them and take them with you wherever you go. One client of mine hangs her lists around her bathroom mirror so that they greet her every morning!

Write about what liberating your dream means.

Write about what, at this point, you understand your dream to be.

Why do you want to realize your fullest potential?

The changes you are willing to make in yourself will alter your life in many ways. Describe how.

Opening the Door to a New Dream

What are the changes you are willing to make in your present situation?

Rejoice. By making your wish a dream, you are making it real. Having made these commitments to yourself, you are becoming a new person. You can never return to who you were before. Therefore, what you have written reflects who and where you are right now.

CHAPTER 2

Breaking Free of Old Mindsets

WELCOME TO THE WORLD OF NEW IDEAS . . . *YOURS AMONG THEM!* Before you can go on to develop your thoughts and plans to their fullest, you will probably need to get rid of a number of unsuspected old ideas, habits, and attitudes blocking your way. For instance, have you ever noticed how much each of us focuses on problems? No matter where you turn, friends, newscasters, and reporters are discussing difficulties with health care, immigration, crime, disease, and national and international debt. Yet, despite our concern—and all the brainpower being devoted to solving these problems—the world's difficulties are *flourishing*. Like our leaders, each of us can easily become overwhelmed by the amount of "fixing" there is to do *out there*. Well, the solution is not to fix mismanagement, waste, greed, or stupidity, although many are trying to do so. The solution to old problems lies in developing new ideas, some based upon the successes and failures of the past—others based upon entirely fresh perspectives. In new approaches lay opportunities to developing *workable procedures and prototypes.* And this is where you come in, because we can no longer continue to use old methods and materials—however successful they may have been in the past.

What we need is for each of us to observe old and new problems from entirely different points of view.

Examining Old Mindsets

Every day, someone accomplishes the inconceivable. Severely injured, a professional skier needed to recover completely before heading back into competition. But once physically healed, she knew that she had to do more than just repeat earlier performances. This time, she had to conquer fears that she'd never had before the accident. That meant—to return to serious competition—she would also have to move *beyond* old limitations established by previous successes. How does an athlete move beyond mental limitations of prior wins? She did it by creating an *entirely new* experience—by going skydiving! Then, having viewed the mountain from a wholly new perspective, she was able to confidently compete again. While she didn't win her next race, she took a quantum leap in preparing for her next race. And the one after that.

Take a minute right now to ask yourself: What restricting ideas or mindsets are holding me back—former failures? The world's present understanding of quantum physics—our current belief that nothing is faster than the speed of light? That for every winner there must be at least one loser? I'm too inexperienced? I'm too old? I'm not important enough for important people to listen to me? Well, guess what: none of those beliefs may be valid!

Seven years ago, no one outside the San Diego area had ever heard of me, but I knew that what I'd learned could improve people's lives. Despite never having written a book, without owning a word processor or typewriter (indeed I can't type—but I dictate real well!) without knowing one thing about writing or publishing, I wrote a book, had it published—then wrote a second book and had it published. Now, my third book is being published . . . along with companion workbooks for all three. Who was I? No one known well enough to be considered important! How did I do it? By constantly working toward my own highest development, which started with teaching, inventing, and administering programs. By biting the bullet and going back to school. By using what I'd learned to take the next step of creating journaling workshops where I helped people define their lives and build better ones. By taking those experiences and sharing what I knew with others through books. *If I can do that, you can achieve your dream, too!*

Embracing New Viewpoints

Each of us is confronted from time to time with small and/or big portions of ourselves that no longer function as well as we'd like. What that tells us is that it is time to find new ways of doing things. But to identify those malfunctioning, or outgrown, parts of ourselves that need to be thrown out, we need to take another look back to see how we were influenced in the past. That's because we are sometimes hauling around stuff that we don't even realize hampers us. And often, that "stuff" is the result of a single event or comment. So, now is the time to re-evaluate what needs to be thrown away.

My client Ellie reviewed a list I compiled of beliefs and feelings established in childhood that can influence our adult lives. Ellie reported that, days later, a thought surfaced. "It seemed to rise right out of my right shoulder," she said. "And it traveled up over my head and announced, 'Boys always win!' Now, where the hell," she asked, "did that come from?" The answer to her question arrived while dreaming a few nights later.

Once again, Ellie was back in junior high, being approached by female teachers who were urging her to run for school president against the most popular and intelligent boy in eighth grade. "We want you to give Jim a run for his money," they said. Now, had my client listened, she would have heard the disclaimer: her teachers had no hope that she would win . . . only that she would "give Jim a run for his money." Confidently, my client enlisted friends, made dozens of posters, prepared and gave her speech . . . and lost the election. Had she been hurt, I asked her. No.

Had she been angry? No.

Then, how had she felt? "Surprised," she answered. "Mystified! I'd never lost anything before. And how could I lose when I'd committed myself so completely, and worked so hard to win?" But "before" had been in elementary school. In factory towns of the fifties, different rules applied for teenagers and adults. From junior high on up, tradition dictated that boys hold all important offices, except secretary. Secretaries were always girls.

"So," I asked. "How has the belief that boys always win restricted you?" She wasn't sure. But in the days that followed, Ellie found her thoughts returning to that question again and again. During our next visit, she observed that she had frequently been asked to run for public office. Always, she had refused; the last thing she wanted or needed, she believed, was to compete in a public arena. Yet she willingly designed brochures and worked for supervisorial, mayoral, and school board candidates. And, in addition to being an educator, she was an author and a museum curator. But, *run for office?* Absolutely not!

"What are you going to do the next time you are asked?" I questioned.

"Well, we'll never know," she laughed. "I'm too old, and we live in the county. There are few public offices in a county system!" Well, you can imagine her surprise when she was asked, only weeks later, to assume a recently vacated seat on a county planning group. Totally committed to getting beyond the old mindset that had, until now, kept her from fulfilling her potential, Ellie accepted. In the next election her name will be on the ballot when she runs for the seat. Already, she has been assured that she will be supported by prestigious homeowners groups and political factions. Where is all this going? Ellie doesn't have the vaguest idea. She only feels that she must do this, even though it is stepping into a void she has avoided for over forty years. So, what old "can't" or "not" is holding you back? Isn't it time to take a new look at the situation? As I've said, once these old unconscious limitations have been examined and reassessed, each of us can then *consciously* decide to change direction and take charge of the future.

Finding the Flaw

When my children were younger, I sewed a great deal. Part of that was from necessity, the other because I enjoyed the piece-by-piece, stitch-by-stitch routine after dealing with rambunctious children all day. But, what drove me crazy was finishing a project, only to discover that I'd failed to do something right. Dealing with a flawed garment—or a flawed dream—can be more than discouraging; sometimes it is fatal to the whole process. That's why it is necessary to do a step-by-step re-evaluation of all the leftover "can'ts" and "nots" that might be around.

Try this experiment: on the large art pad I suggested you buy, make a cluster diagram of everything that might be holding you back from pursuing your dream.

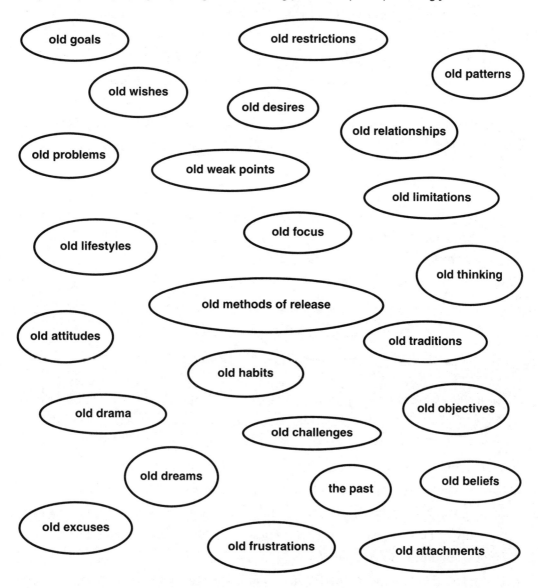

Having restrictions down on paper makes it easier to see earlier decisions you've come to regret or question. When you've identified every limiting factor that you know, look them over to see if anything is missing. By recognizing what's in your way, you can attend to it. You might want to include in your diagram: adequate financing, unresolved issues, family members, friends, inadequate preparation, incomplete accreditation, lack of self-awareness, fear of success, making wrong choices.

Now, select one particular area that you want to examine more closely. For example, consider "old attitudes." Using this as a focus, create a second cluster diagram that helps you more specifically identify what your old attitudes are.

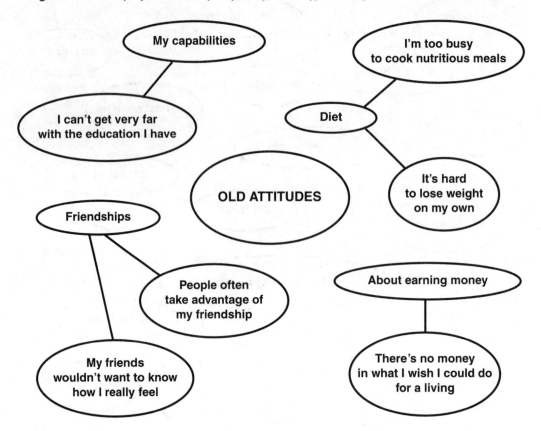

For instance, if you listed "fear of not having adequate financing" as an old attitude, you can clarify it by recalling when you first experienced not having enough money. Were you nine and fearful that you wouldn't have enough to get into a movie? Did you worry that you might not have enough money to buy your mother something for Mother's Day? On a first date, when you worried that your date might order too much food? Or was it when your parents couldn't afford to pay for something you really wanted? Follow your feelings of fear back to their beginnings. Remember what you did to get beyond the fear that time. What can you do to get beyond it this time? You can't, after all, allow old fears to limit you now!

Having completed this second diagram, you can view some of the notions that may be holding you back. Now you can consciously choose to release limiting ideas and conditions. But you must first replace them from a totally new viewpoint.

To do that, make a third diagram. In it, select new attitudes to replace each of your former beliefs in the second diagram. Remember, you are viewing old limitations in an entirely new way. So, just as you cannot return to your childhood home and see it in the same way as you did then, revisit each remembered former belief or attitude from a completely new vantage point.

By using this identification and replacement technique, you break through each of those barriers keeping you from using your full power to accomplish what you want. So, congratulate yourself. And expect unexpected shifts in your everyday understanding of "the way things ought to be" to emerge—the result of casting light into your mind's previously shadowed nooks and corners. By consciously exposing outdated constraints, you begin to release the power to create your highest dreams. But, is there another piece of the puzzle?

Breaking Free of Old Mindsets

Imagine that you have in front of you pieces of a puzzle to illustrate all the wishes and dreams that you have already realized. Trace or duplicate this puzzle on your art pad. Leave one puzzle piece blank, and label the rest with your successes.

Now, examine those pieces and acknowledge yourself! What process did you go through to complete those dreams? Isn't it interesting how, although they are separate and distinct in themselves, they fit together? How did each dream relate to the others—sequentially? Independently? Does that suggest anything about the unlabeled piece of the puzzle? What label do you think you want to put there?

Now, review your puzzle and in the blank puzzle piece write what you want to experience to complete your current dream.

Whether or not you have identified the missing piece, recognize the joys that you have already experienced. Reflection and review are always helpful when facing new challenges. In fact, like life and learning, they are ongoing processes. In other words, repetition is essential for growth. Repeat these exercises as often as you need—just as you play and replay your favorite music, reread your favorite books, or watch—for the umpteenth time, your favorite movies. Everything that we love should be revisited and reviewed so that we might reacquaint ourselves with beauty and happiness and joy . . . and to alert us to any nuances we might have missed.

Moving Beyond Perceived Limitations

We cannot allow ourselves to limit our dreams based upon past experiences—negative *or* positive. Even those of us who think we have worked through earlier obstacles often retain vestiges of old hurts and failures. You may have attained many of your dreams by healing some of those wounds: coming from a dysfunctional family, living in poverty, or simply having had little, or no opportunity to be powerful. Knowing, as an adult, that it was your *choice* to either dwell in days gone by or use those experiences to grow and expand, you chose to grow. However, even if your parents merely quenched your investigative spirit, you may have some ghost messages to remove from your unconscious—questions or statements like, Who do you think you are . . .

✳ Queen of Sheba/King of Siam?

✳ God's gift to women?

Breaking Free of Old Mindsets

* Some kind of hotshot?

* Mrs. Got Rocks?

* Mr. Big Shot?

* Little Miss Know-It-All?

* Miss Goody Two-Shoes

* Miss Fancy Pants?

* A Dreamer?

Were you told that dreamers never accomplished anything, that if you were going to get anywhere it was time to pull your head out of the clouds? And how many of you were told that only fools look for pie in the sky?

As a child, it is unlikely that you replied, "Why, yes, that's absolutely right—I *am* the Queen of Sheba," but you can now. You can say, "I *do* know it all. I am a dreamer, and dreamers are perfectly capable of keeping their feet on the ground while their heads are in the clouds! As a dreamer, *I am supposed* to beat my own drum in a rhythm all my own!"

Take time right now to make a list of every limiting statement you have ever been told. Include all the messages you've ever received about what you can't possibly do or become. When you finish, go back and underline the statements you heard that stopped you in your tracks. If other forgotten messages surface later, be sure to add them to your list so that you will not allow them to limit you again.

While those limitations are an important chapter in your book of life, they must be put on the shelf for now. Don't deny that which has gotten you to this point, but allowing it to influence your decisions can diminish your forward movement, if you allow it to do so. Instead, embrace your history. Build strength in your broken parts. Then, step aside and move on! And from now on, when someone asks you the equivalent of "Who do you think you are—the Queen of Sheba," answer firmly:

More—I'm a dreamer. Before anything becomes reality,
the idea must be born. And I dream wonderful things

and commit myself to work toward bringing my dreams
into reality for the benefit of us all!

By doing this, you give yourself permission to change. In not permitting that change, we hobble ourselves with someone else's beliefs. Like domestic elephants, we continue to be inhibited by early training. Baby elephants, as you may recall, are chained by one leg to a stake that allows them only a fixed range of movement. Even when the connecting chain is removed, the metal anklet that remains prevents them from knowing they are free. Too often, we accept parameters established for us by authority figures in our childhood.

Within days of entering preschool or kindergarten, most of us gave up a good measure of our natural spontaneity, energy, and drive. "Don't daydream," you were told, teaching you that paying attention to authority is far more important than dreaming. Then you learned the importance of sitting quietly in your seat, gaining permission to go to the bathroom, and walking, not running, in the hall. It didn't take you long to learn the advantages of earning the teacher's good will, and soon you were spending most of your energy becoming an adult's definition of a "good" boy or girl. Certainly, some limitations are necessary for every child as he or she grows into adulthood. But the truth is, the main reason that most children are stripped of their instinctive energy and enthusiasm is that most adults don't believe that individual vigor or power is convenient—or even possible—*for ordinary people*. (Sure, the King of Siam's kids can be loud and demanding, but who told you that you were a prince?) So, in America, we grow up thinking it is more desirable to be popular with friends and approved of by "higher-ups" than to reactivate our natural power. Then, to make sure that our children are as successful as we are, we require the same compromising things of them that were required of us.

Untying the Knots of Forgotten Perceptions

As a former teacher, a mother, and a grandmother, I confess that life is quieter and more orderly when we subdue the natural instincts of children. But, oh, what we lose when we suppress a child's spontaneous delight in learning.

And, what adults lose by not realizing that they *need* to reclaim their natural power when they grow up. In part, that is because the limitations we have lived with have become so comfortable that we sometimes forget that we've outgrown them. We don't know that, once again, we can trust ourselves to express who we really are. In forgetting, we have denied ourselves the thrill of exploration and discovery, the satisfaction of growth, and the joy of celebrating the appropriate uses of power.

"But," you say, "I understand all of that, and I am still feeling reluctant. Maybe because the size of this new dream is intimidating." Well, if your dream is large, then it is possible that the reluctance you feel is a result of some old "nots."

The "nots" that you accept may be so firmly embedded in your thinking process that you've never questioned them. Those "nots" cause anxiety. They drain your energy. They sabotage your progress. Think of these "nots" as knots. Just as you can't jump a knotted rope, or fashion an attractive bow from twisted ribbon, you can't be your most *powerful* self if you are knotting up your own creative flow! Here is a list to consider—it may lead you to discover just how your perceptions might be obstructing your progress.

Notice what each phrase "says" to you, and when one describes you, circle it:

Not passionate	Pretending not to know	Not loving
Not working	Not taking responsibility	Not prepared
Not knowing	Not risking	Not enough time
Not willing	Not changing	Not taking action
Not fit enough	Not learning	Not taking time
Not prepared	Not celebrating	Not enough energy
Not capable	Not smart enough	Not nice enough
Not right	Not interested	Not talented
Not polite	Not educated enough	Not pretty/handsome
Not safe	Not doing what makes my heart sing/spirit fly	Not a priority
Not important	Not significant	Not fun

Not focused	Not efficient	Not assertive
Not tough enough	Not tactful	Not effective
Not rich enough	Not cultured enough	Not understanding
Not good enough	Not neat enough	Not organized
Not thin enough	Not experienced	Not valuable
Not worthy	Not enough encouragement	Not reaching out
Not enough money	Not enough money to learn	Not telling the truth
Not practicing what I know	Not enough money to celebrate	Not confident
Not exciting	Not in a good mood, or good enough mood	Not happy enough
Not choosing to be with other celebrants and dreamers		Not dreaming my biggest dream

Not _____ (add your own personal nots)

Make a copy of your encircled "nots" list and post it where you will see it every day. When you identify any additional "nots," add them to your list. Then note in your journal, workbook, or pad of paper, those changes you can make to start untangling those knots. Describe how you can begin making those changes that allow you to activate your dreams by pulling you closer to the position in which you belong.

Liberating Your Limitations

For example, if you are "not happy," break free from that limitation by writing about what it feels like to be happy!

Right now, list and describe those times you have been happy, and what it would take for you to be happy right now. Specify where that happiness could lead you. List your options to reach that place. Determine what would free you to do what you need to do. Write down what you need to make that a reality. You might draw a picture of yourself on your art pad just enjoying being there.

This process jump-starts you out of the "nots." Whenever you remove one of these blocks, it's like opening the floodgates of a dam. Suddenly, your life has the freedom to surge ahead. Feel that emancipation? *If not, these examples might help.* Say, for instance, that you cannot get beyond "not in a good/good enough mood." What worked in the past to lift you out of a bad mood? Did you feel it dissipating by taking a walk, watching a sunrise or sunset, exercising, lighting a candle, listening to music, soaking in a tub of hot water, getting a massage, talking with a friend?

List those things you've done in the past. Review your list and choose one to activate. Right now!

Say that you circled "not risking." Remember the successful risks you have already taken? Think about the growth you made by taking them. Now, consider your next risky steps.

Write about the ways you can prepare yourself to make them successful, too.

What if you identified "not telling the truth"? First, figure out if it is a faulty truth that you have been hanging on to. As an adult you might find that the "truths" you accepted as a child are now merely a child's perception of an adult situation or attitude.

List those long-held truths. Ask yourself: What is true for me right now?

If you identified "not enough money" as the reason for not following your dreams, listen to yourself. Trust the messages your subconscious mind gives you. You might now realize that you could cut back on what you have believed until now to be essential expenditures.

Now, make a list of expenses that could be trimmed, or halted.

And if you listed "not changing" as one of your nots and you know that change was, and is, necessary—trust that it is time to move forward. In other words, stop waiting—begin making those small and large changes that add up to important progress.

Having completed, and contemplated upon, the preceding exercises, know that you are moving right along. But be watchful as you continue along your way. Be on the alert for the "not" traps that would pull you away from your destination. Catch yourself whenever you even suspect a "not." Then turn it into a learning experience.

Each time you recognize and avoid a "not," record what you did to circumvent it, and how it kept your forward motion intact. Make a record of those experiences. In each case, chronicle how you experienced your power, and how you expressed it. Untying, or going beyond, the knots is not a one-time exercise, so use those successful situations to guide you beyond those "nots" in the future.

Accepting No Limits: Think Big, Think High

Know that you are a transformative force in this interconnected world and accept no limits to what you can be or contribute. Elevate your thinking by considering some of the most far-reaching dreams in human history. And remember, most started in searches for solutions to practical problems: the Pyramids; elaborate canal systems in ancient China, Egypt, and nineteenth century New York State; the Sistine Chapel; Beethoven's Ninth Symphony; the cotton gin; electricity; the combustion engine; automobiles; flight; wonder drugs; television; Disneyland; and computers. Monthly, new products and services astonish us. What *hasn't* changed in the last two thousand years is the way individuals and nations perceive one another—we still see each other as "them, and us." Business and governmental structures haven't changed either; nor the view that for every winner there must be a loser, or that an army is for conquering and controlling rather than actively teaching and illustrating to foreign populaces and governments the principles of democracy and fairness. Of course, that would require that *our* military be formally instructed in the ideals of democratic process. Old warhorses are unlikely to change their views, but there is hope from younger generations.

Yet, just for fun, let's go straight for world-shaking results by doing the following exercise. . . .

Breaking Free of Old Mindsets

Take a blank piece of paper and entitle it "Pie in the Sky Dreams." Draw outlines of clouds all over it. And inside each cloud log in some of the most ingenious inventions, concepts, and accomplishments in the world to date. Did you identify with any of them? Remember that!

Pie in the Sky Dreams

Now, go deep into your inner knowing self to lift your dreams and thoughts higher. Ask: Why am I here on this planet at this time in history? What was I born to create—or continue? What am I going to leave as my legacy?

On another page write the title "My Pie in the Sky Dreams." Draw at least twelve clouds. Inside each, write ideas that can change the world.

As you recorded your "pie in the sky" dreams, did you go back to a particular point in time when, for you, they were still very real possibilities? How do they correspond to the dreams you have already accomplished? How do they relate to the dream you are working on now? Or did you diagram your present dream?

If you are finding this difficult, put your pen down and recall all the wishes and hopes and dreams you ever had. Should you need to be reminded or inspired, remember those television programs or articles that continue to demand your attention. What is it about those situations or subjects that appeal to you? Love old John Wayne movies? Is it the actor or the old west that captures you? Does any particular Wayne movie have anything to do with an old dream? What about developments in genetics, negotiations between warring tribes, clans, or countries? Pick up your pen and write anything down that comes to mind. Then, when you've dredged up all that you can, look at what you've written and imagine an inner voice saying, "Not high enough—go beyond. Dream higher! A lot higher!" Finish this sentence: The one dream I am claiming at this moment is. . . . Write it down!

Moving Forward: Growing and Expanding

Vow to do whatever it takes to lift yourself above the mundane activities and thoughts of your everyday world. And, having already scheduled time for inspirational thought, you can now sit back in a favorite place and begin thinking about where you are going. Eyes closed, you begin raising your consciousness, lifting your inner self higher than your head, higher than the treetops. Then, soaring in a cloudless sky you observe that the space you occupy belongs to you and you alone. No one before or after you will inhabit that space. And then it comes to you just how important you and your contributions are—that without you and what only you can do, a vital part of the universe collapses and dies. Comprehending this, you feel a sense of wonder; everything that you are now and ever will be starts here—beyond the perceived confines of what most people in our Western civilization believe. You realize that you can accomplish what needs to be done because not any one of us works alone. When we are working with clarity of purpose, we work with a higher purpose and the more concentrated energy of the universe. Without all those perceptions restricting you in the past, you can move forward into a fuller expression of your powers.

Never Again...

Now that you have completed this chapter, you'll never again have to be restricted by old mindsets. But you *do* have to take care not to fall back into outgrown patterns when facing the unfamiliar. Right here—right now—write about these issues so that you may forever live in choice!

In your everyday life, what have you read that helped you break free of old mindsets?

What have you observed that helped empower you to identify and break free of old mindsets?

List the radio and televisions programs that invited you to examine your thinking . . . your choices.

Describe scenes or list lines in films that mirrored outmoded behaviors and thoughts that you've chosen to reject.

Describe the fictional people who were your heroes and heroines before now.

Describe the real people who have been your heroes and heroines to this point.

Make the Dream Real... Make it Yours

Thoughts and words are real. Both are so powerful that they promote internal and external action. As you use the words you have chosen to live with, you begin to write the script for the rest of your life.

Describe your reality of yourself up until now.

Describe your new reality from this moment on.

Breaking Free of Old Mindsets

To accommodate your transformation, list the new words and conversations you will be using with your friends, family, and co-workers.

Rejoice. By making the dream real, you make it yours. By regularly introducing new words and behaviors into your life, you leave the unworkable behind. The new you is growing.

CHAPTER 3

Living from Your Fullest Spirit Power

HAVING PUT THE CHAPTERS ON DREAMWORK AND RIDDING yourself of old mindsets to practical use, we can move on to clarifying what I mean by "spirit power." What I call spirit power, you might be calling a hunch, gut feeling, sixth sense, intuition, the universal mind, the Force, God, Goddess, Source, Guardian Angel, Higher Self, Higher Power, Inner Power, or Spirit Guide. No matter what the name, what it describes is an energy beyond our conscious self that works with us to recognize and accomplish our dreams. As an energizing higher self, spirit power frees each of us to tap into that part of ourselves that is increasingly expressive, dynamic, independent, and free. By using our spirit power, we begin living in an evolving state of joy and discovery.

Start by reclaiming your child's sense of wonderment over the simplest of things. Allow yourself to rediscover the mystery of a butterfly's flight, the curiosity accompanying the most mundane of activities. Retrain yourself to be open to all of life's possibilities for, when we listen to and heed our own inner knowing, we call our spirit power into action.

How many times have you heard stories of people who backed out of a flight because of a strange uneasiness, and the plane later crashed; the person who was suddenly disquieted about taking their regular route home, only to discover later that by taking an alternate road they'd avoided a serious accident? Or, maybe you made a phone call to someone whose face or name kept popping into your mind—and discovered that he or she was thinking about you, too. Each of those incidents is an illustration of aligning with inner knowing: spirit power. What I recommend that you start doing now is to *consciously and regularly* tap into that power. Doing so allows you to further assume personal responsibility for your past, your present, and a rewarding future. "Tapping in," of course, requires time alone each day during which to think, meditate, and visualize. In an environment that encourages reflective and creative thought, you can put your spirit power to work.

Claiming Your Biggest Dream

Go back and reread the dream you described at the end of the second chapter. Are you ready to refine it—maybe even redefine it?

Let's clarify your dream even further. On your art pad, draw a number of circles. In them, write your thoughts to these questions:

* *Any dreams hidden in my heart?*
* *What circumstances are propelling me into this new territory?*
* *What preparations will I need to make to ready myself for the realization of my dream?*
* *What help will I need from other people?*
* *What help will I need from my spiritual energy?*
* *What financial resources will I need?*
* *How will I use my own personal power as I work toward my dream?*
* *What are any other concerns specific to my dream?*

Just for the fun of it, pretend that the spiritual energy available to you comes in the form of a magical work crew. There they wait, energy in action, ready to do your bidding. At your request, crew members will assist, empower, observe, facilitate, and guide you to claim your highest dream.

Without any notion of how it's going to happen—wipe your mind clear. Taking your time, allow an answer to emerge. Some people actually see the answer written on the inside of their foreheads. Others hear it, others sense it, still others just "know" it. Even if you've never done this before, trust that your inner knowing will supply you with an answer. If not now, pay particular attention to what's being said and going on around you for the next few days. Your answer—and the answer to all your questions—may appear in a dream, in the title of a book glimpsed on a newsstand, or in a word spoken on television or in the subway. However and whenever the answers come, jot them down.

I always experience a real lightheartedness following each answer. Your sense of knowing may have you feeling it, too—or you may experience other physical or mental signs that you are gaining additional clarity about what you want, why you want it, and how you can get it. Thank those energies, and ask them to keep working.

One of my clients tried this out and inspired herself to even greater aspiration by asking experts of the past to enter into her creative imagination times. Along with her "magical crew" she would utilize the collective unconscious by asking authors, inventors, artists, politicians, spiritual leaders, and the like to enter into this designing/brainstorming/free association time. She shared she had once asked famous architect Frank Lloyd Wright to assist her in planning her mediation room and the resultant ideas were truly magical.

Now, transcribe your answers, whether they make sense or not, onto your art pad. Add subcategories when related ideas come to you. Draw connecting lines showing any possible relationships. Select a colored pen that matches your enthusiasm and encircle those tasks that you can joyfully embrace and accomplish by yourself. In a different energizing hue, encircle those tasks you will turn over to your magical work crew to manifest.

Claiming My Biggest Dream

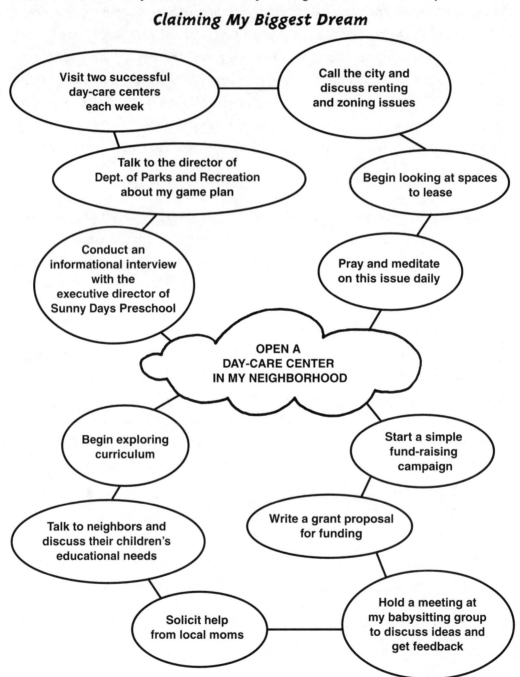

Don't limit yourself by trying to figure out how your magical work crew will accomplish their tasks. Trust their supportive energy to accomplish these tasks with perfect timing.

Having reclaimed and/or redefined your highest dream, understand that it may take some time to assimilate what has emerged. So, relax. Take several days, or weeks, to embrace what you and your magical crew are on your way to accomplishing. Take along your journal. When the mood strikes, record your thoughts and actions. Enjoy the journey that you have begun, dream activator.

Higher Dreams—Universal Endeavors

Even if you know exactly what your dream is, there is no need to rush out and accomplish it in three weeks. Look upon this time of integration as a valuable investment of time in yourself. Use these days or weeks to *think*— and write—to better understand what you need to do, and want to do—to prepare yourself for this next stage in your life. Although you may continue living in the same house, same city, and/or same country, you are in a different place, now. You will want to become familiar with it before venturing further.

Begin by asking yourself this question: How will the realization of my dream impact the universe?

Like great dreamers before you, you don't have to grasp everything before you begin, but you do need to see that your dream reaches beyond your own personal gain. Say that you want to be a world-class tennis player—recognize that you will do more than bring thrills and inspiration to millions of like-minded hopefuls around the world. Your involvement in the industry will support tennis tournaments, sponsors, underwriters, and advertising agencies, which provide employment to thousands of people from executives to sign painters and ticket takers. Your dream enriches many!

Ask: What do I need to do to prepare myself for what is to come?

Living from Your Fullest Spirit Power

Simply *thinking* about these things takes you above your own personal mountain for a new view of your potential. Contemplation provides space for new growth and expansion. Still, maybe you haven't extended it enough.

Read the following, then ask yourself, How far have I extended my limits? Is my dream big or high enough—or do I need to rise even higher?

In every area in which anyone has talent, expertise, and interest, there is a higher dream waiting to be realized. The following dreamers have plans in different stages of completion, but in the acts of being conceptualized and spoken, the dreamers' dreams evolved from thinking about and recording their dreams-in-action. You may enjoy reading what some other dreamers are thinking about, and claiming, as they solidify their dreams. The following initial dream statements were in response to my question: "If you had three wishes, what would the only one be?" When you have finished reading their answers, invite your spirit power to help you release your creativity to answer that same question.

This first dream statement was made by a well-seasoned speech writer in Alaska. Ready to incorporate all of who she had become through the many jobs she had held, she wanted to move into an entirely new life through the realization of a new dream.

> My plan is to promote caring connection between people
> through international trade. My import-export business
> will support individual creativity and giftedness among
> local artists in many cultures.

A social worker wanted to improve the system in which she works by doing the following:

> I want to practice and teach a psychosocial approach in
> medicine nationally to impact physicians to become
> more in tune with the spirit and drive of their patients,
> while celebrating the whole human experience.

A hair stylist wanted to provide more for her clients than just superior hair service. By developing her own spirituality, she could inspire them toward achieving the same deep sense of inner peace.

> My dream is to live from a state of inner peace and happiness. As I achieve this, I will become a giver of light, a shining star, using my talents to their full potential.

A wealthy housewife penned:

> I plan to form a network of women spanning the globe and crossing cultures. The impact will be constructive and positive, inspiring and joyful, quiet and gentle.

A multitalented psychologist, fearing to take a chance on herself, wrote:

> I will fully express myself as a channel for the light by being a well-paid published author of works that combine humor, healing, and spirit.

Because she knows of the connection between a beautiful environment and spirituality, a prominent wine consultant wants to provide a place that will allow others to tap into the power of the human spirit.

> To provide a Napa Valley spiritual center where world leaders in decision-making positions will come to solve problems that impact people all over the world.

Another psychologist, reaching a point of increasing clarity, started with the following:

> I plan to bring the concepts of personal transformation into the business community. Through a thriving consultation and seminar practice, travel, and a

Living from Your Fullest Spirit Power

79

published book and series of relaxation tapes, I will bring the people-related skills learned in my clinical practice to the general work world, enabling people to communicate more effectively and experience their interconnectedness both within themselves (body, mind, and spirit) and with each other.

Arlene, a teacher from Kokomo, Indiana, who views life as wonderful, wants to help teens feel the same way. She wrote:

I want to build a business that gives me the opportunity to have a positive impact on a million-plus lives—a personal image and personal growth consulting business that helps others live their dreams. The impact will be more joy, peace, love, and happiness. People will once again whistle while they work, and learn that it's OK to have a good time.

Other dream activators center on improving themselves. The importance of this cannot be overemphasized because the changes we make in ourselves have a direct positive influence on so many others. The personal investment you make in becoming whole and complete cannot help but affect those around you—and then around them. Eventually, all individual learning and personal growth influences the world. Just imagine what is happening right now because the following dream has been activated!

I want to celebrate being at peace within myself, to be a nonanxious presence to others, and to encourage and empower others to find and live from that deep place of peace, too. I am the wife of a corporate executive and mother of two adult sons. While I pursued my own career as artist, writer, and teacher, I found being superwoman increasingly debilitating. Burnt out and suffering from depression, I moved from being driven by outer dictates to living from a deeper spiritual level. As I trust my creative spirit, I am able to be more open, honest, and authentic with myself and others and as I care for myself, I am able to be a healing presence to others. My life is now a comfortable balance between being and doing. Like the old song says, "Let there be peace on earth, and let it begin with me!"

The universe calls each of us to be the very best we can be; to give the best of ourselves, to inspire others to help us use our power to attain our highest dreams. The following statement took me out of the ordinary and served as a reminder that this is where I want to live all of the time. How about you? Getting in touch with the largeness of oneself is "mystical, marvelous, magnificent, and mysterious, too!"

Unfortunately, not everyone lives there—or feels much hope of doing so! This is a classic illustration of the broken spirits of individuals, and nations, as well.

In Yugoslavia, an engineer whose skills were no longer in demand during his nation's turmoil took a job as a tour guide. In this way, he could make some money while sharing with others the country he loves. I asked him why he felt his nation was in such serious trouble. "The trouble with my country is," he said, "that the people have given up their dreams." That is true in many areas of the world today. And compelling evidence exists to support his conclusions.

In our country, too, the spirit of citizens is being tested as it hasn't been since the Great Depression of the 1930s. Now, more than ever, each of us must believe in our own individual importance within the grand scheme of things—even if we cannot visualize that scheme in its entirety. So, don't compromise—believe in yourself, and make the changes necessary to have your dream come true!

In improving our own condition, we can better the lot of those around us. I don't want to make this sound easy, or without risk or setbacks. What I do want to say is that, despite sensible reasons for doubt—and maybe even despair—you must retain a passionate optimism while facing your realities. Consciously looking on the bright side allows us to select what is possible instead of giving in to

Living from Your Fullest Spirit Power

hopelessness and helplessness. What we knew as youngsters is true—each of us is responsible for our own destiny! We may have given that control to others for a time, but—as adults—we need not continue doing so. For that very reason, I make an effort to associate with people whose futuristic ideas I admire.

I make it a point to surround myself with these practical and creative idealists because, together, each of us is more than we are alone. Together, we share ideas and fine tune them, exposing one another to the process of working toward the highest good of all. Those people I have come to admire most are those who recognize that it is not only futile, but globally self-destructive, to continue resuscitating worn-out nineteenth century institutions and procedures. In these final few years of the twentieth century we *must* explore new ways of viewing and doing *everything*. For instance, after the 1993 Los Angeles earthquake, the unthinkable happened. Because employees couldn't get to work, companies allowed those with home computers to work at home. Guess what? Not only had employers found a new way of working through a crisis, working at home proved to be more effective for many workers than coming into the office! How many earth-shaking events do we need before we begin improving our outmoded systems?

In meeting with other progressive thinkers in science, social services, politics, business, government, and the arts, I am privy to learning new ways of replacing obsolete practices, and of using innovative procedures to revitalize tired infrastructures. From this will emerge a more enlightened workforce in which individuals increasingly assume total responsibility for themselves and their own dreams. But, other inventions, methods, ideas, and approaches are needed, too. Maybe *yours*! Are you regularly setting aside at least fifteen minutes each day to align with your dream—to think about it, visualize it, *live* it?

Unleashing Your Mental Energy

There is immense energy released simply by *imagining* an empowered populace. Envisioned, those people who are intent upon nurturing responsible self-fulfillment can replace a society bogged down in meting out punishment to miscreants. Pictured, a world where governments sponsor machines of peace instead of war can happen. So, visualize the rebuilding of our aging roads and bridges generating as many jobs as it takes to produce increasingly arcane methods of nuclear mayhem.

Each of us wants to live in peace and harmony. None of us want gangs of teenagers to represent a threat to each other or the rest of us. We don't want there to be a need for more jails for juveniles or adults. What personal action can *you* take to bring more peace and harmony to yourself, to your home, to your community and workplace, that will effect change in the way things are now? If you are a parent, what can you do to give positive direction to kids in your neighborhood? How effective are after-school activities in your community? If you are a businessperson, what can you do to improve the availability of clubs and activities? What can you do if you are a priest, a minister, a policeman or policewoman, a board member of the gardening society, or a retired person? First of all, find out what is already provided. How can it be improved? What action can you take to help? What if community colleges taught self-awareness and higher consciousness to everyone involved in after-school programs and organizations? They, in turn, could teach caregivers to teach children to fulfill themselves in a healthy and peaceful way. With consciously aware people teaching others how to fulfill themselves, everybody wins! Just imagine: less crime, fewer homeless, fewer throw-away children, and more people capable of caring about others because they've learned appropriate ways of loving themselves.

So there is much to do, dream activator. After the age of three, we learned to protect or hide our creative and spirit energies. Are you still guarding yours because of old fears surrounding revealing your inner self? Or are you afraid that someone will steal your ideas? Do you fear that being more than you appear would threaten your job? Cost you friends? Hurt your family? To unleash and use spiritual and mental energies, you must begin moving beyond doubt and fear. By choosing to do something positive with the experiences of your past, you move to a higher place—and by doing so, you lift your part of the universe. Let me illustrate this by telling a story about myself.

Accepting Personal Power

Some years ago I was at a school board meeting where it became clear that my opinions were not wanted. It was a new experience: I'd been a master teacher for years, developed innovative classroom procedures, had trained many student teachers for K-6 classrooms all over the country—indeed, had designed and operated a school based upon openness, creativity, and encouraging children to assume personal responsibility for their thoughts and actions. Now, elected non-educators didn't want to hear what I had to say? Suddenly, I knew what it felt like to be powerless—and I didn't like it one bit. Who among us wants to be where we are not valued—where what we must do is diametrically opposed to our instincts and training? That became the first uncomfortable night of many.

For weeks, I struggled with my feelings of hurt, dismissal, confusion, and fear—you know, the usual steps in the decision-making process. You see, I loved everything about teaching; the kids, the smell of chalk, the personal and profession chatter in the teachers room. Yet, a mental chafing told me that it was time to move on. What I needed, I decided, was to leave teaching and go back to college for an additional degree in psychology so that I could begin counseling adults. This would allow me to upgrade my educational experiences and skills for use with an older audience. However, although it took only the last few sentences to explain my decision process, please don't think that it came easily. Changing even one part of my life seriously impacted my relationship with my husband and our four children. It also significantly challenged our family income and health insurance coverage. Yet I was just fine—until the day I packed up my teaching supplies for the last time. Then, I went through what I call the "crazies"—which is nothing but unreasoning *fear*. What was I doing, I asked myself—leaving a well-paying job that I adored? And even though I knew that the new place I was heading would bring me even more joy, what was it going to take to get there? Fortunately, my fear was only momentary, because fear is simply a lack of clarity or focus. And I knew where I was going!

Even with clarity, however, it was not easy to return to school. Yet, despite juggling school, youth sports, money, and housekeeping schedules, the family and I made it. And that is because, from the moment I realized that I had outgrown my former profession, I also understood that my response to the changing focus in education was just the nudge I needed to move on. Understanding the process allowed me to activate myself, which put me back into my own power. Knowing this made doing the school work and interning for thousands of hours a marvelous experience. From there, I went on to establish a personal growth consulting business, then to author and have published two books and related workbooks, and then to establish the Live Your Dream organization. That is what I want for you: to be able to recognize what it is that drains your personal and spirit energy; to move beyond it; to experience the thrill of going within to reacquaint yourself with the source of those powers; to receive inner direction; to feel the exhilaration that comes from discovering, and working toward, your highest dreams, and the satisfaction of having done so.

Altering Outmoded Concepts of Power

Our understanding of power comes not only from observation, but from listening to the stories and directions of earlier generations. Many people don't go for their really big dreams because they perceive such an action to be selfish, or self-centered. That's why they turn their personal power over to family members, friends, or employers. Others, frequently those who were physically, verbally, and/or emotionally abused as children, grow up determined to do unto others as was done unto them. These are the power-grabbers who must be king of the mountain, who consistently keep everyone else below them to maintain a position at the top. As different as they are, both *misuses* of power limit an individual's ability to move ahead.

So, are you holding yourself back because you fear your own powers? A friend once confessed, "My God, if I let go of all the power that's in me, I'd blow everyone else off the planet!" Truly believing that, she deliberately kept from going forth with her deepest held dream. Instead, she devoted her superior organizational skills and intelligence to community projects. This is not to suggest that community projects are unsuitable as highest dreams. They just weren't hers!

The power feared by my friend, the queen of community projects, was the result of her rearing. "Don't be smarter than the boys," her mother warned. "You'll never get anything that way!" Note that mother said "anything" not "anywhere," because 99 percent of the women of her generation had nowhere

Living from Your Fullest Spirit Power

85

to go except into marriage. Only poor women had jobs. Only a rare few middle- and upper-class women were educated to become doctors or lawyers. Fewer still were those women who were nationally and internationally known and respected—Congresswoman Millicent Fenwick of New Jersey, who served from the 1930s to the late 1980s as an author, congresswoman, ambassador, and U.S. advisor on civil rights, was a rare exception. All other women concentrated upon getting "things" from their male providers. Just so does my friend continue to carry her 1940s/1950s fear of being so aggressive that she might offend men and be ostracized by other women. No matter that she encouraged her daughters to tackle the professional male world. My friend remains a victim of fears instilled in her when she was a teenager. Those fears must be examined, then dissipated, if she is ever to use her power appropriately and fully.

Assuming Total Responsibility

Most people carry their fear of one or more parents into adulthood. How do we acknowledge their power over us? At one extreme by imitating them, at the other by consciously behaving contrary to their behavior. Both are examples of abandoning powers that are rightfully ours as adults to an old relationship. Unfortunately, it's like an old, familiar dance—with each partner knowing the steps so well he or she doesn't even question them.

Margi had a dominating father who dismissed her every opinion as "silly." By the age of sixteen, she had learned that, if she wanted her father to like her, she would have to keep her ideas to herself. Now, at thirty, she has had a series of romances that died when she was unable to tell her suitors what she wanted from their relationship. Even in the 1990s, most women are terrified that people won't like them if they assert even a little power. So, while Margi's father had no conscious plan to turn his teenager into an uncommunicative adult, that is what he did. That he continues to disagree with everything she says is, in a perverse way, his attempt to keep her a dependent little girl. What he doesn't realize is that she despises herself for not having the courage to talk back to him. Before she can get on with her life, she must demand that he allow her opinions to be voiced. Then, she must start relationships off by letting the other person know what she likes, dislikes, and expects. Doing this firmly, but in a nonthreatening way, will take time and work, but it will activate her own personal and spiritual powers.

The unwillingness to assume these powers is not limited to women. A man came to one of my workshops; he wanted his wife to accompany him, but she had "too much to do" to participate. It was as if her need to keep a spotless house and dinner on the table at 5:00 P.M. was more important than anything that he wanted to do. At lunchtime I gave the group an assignment to get in touch with paying attention to every moment . . . and then to record what was going on. The man went home for lunch and, because he had enjoyed the morning, asked his wife to come back with him. "It would be fun for both of us to be tapping into this experience," he reported himself as saying. Her response had been: "Well, I can't. I have to fix a casserole for dinner!"

How's that for letting him know that fixing a meal is more important than going with him? What he said upon returning was, "So I came back alone, because I suddenly remembered how many times she has used this excuse not to do things." What he wrote was that he finally understood that her unwillingness to join him was more than a rejection of a single event they might have shared. It was her unwillingness to join him in revitalizing their final years together.

In my "Write Your Life" workshops I tell people that it is important to record your life, but not relive it. That's because there is no power in reliving a situation that you cannot change. It is a temptation, when reviewing our lives, to get all caught up in re-experiencing events where we failed, or were used, or even abused. But the world—and we—have changed. In earlier years, we might not have been as secure or confident as we are now. So, now we would not deal with that situation in the same way. So, it is essential not to reactivate old feelings of powerlessness and anger. Instead, when we look back, it is important to note the progress in ourselves in dealing with potentially dangerous or harmful situations. In this way, we do not relinquish the confidence we have developed over the years by meeting and mastering many of life's challenges.

As I said these things to my audience, a woman in her sixties listened to me with growing alarm. As I explained that it was necessary to go back and

Living from Your Fullest Spirit Power

reacquaint ourselves with earlier dreams we either manifested or forgot, she became quite agitated. Tentatively, she raised her hand. Was I saying, she wanted to know, that she should take a closer look at what she had wanted before she was raising children, taking care of her husband, and busying herself with club work? Yes, I nodded. And dreams she'd had *while* caring for a family and doing community work.

"I was too busy to dream," she said. Then, after a pause, she asked, "Are you saying that I could make a different life for myself—*now*?"

"As you start looking back over your life," I replied, "you will automatically become more active in planning what kind of life you want in the future. That's because when we evaluate what happened to earlier dreams, we become more conscious of how seldom we really designed the life we are living right now. And one of the steps toward experiencing joy is in *living a life that we have consciously designed.*"

"That's what you're talking about?" she demanded. "Joy? You mean being joyful all the time—every *day*?"

"What a wonderful question," I laughed. Then, going to the right side of the chalkboard, I wrote the word "Joy." Walking across the room to the left side of the board, I drew an arrow running all the way to "Joy." Above the sheath of the arrow, I wrote the words: "sadness, trial, pain, loss, discomfort, death."

"These," I said, "are the human experiences each of us goes through to get to adult states of *joy*. Please notice that the arrow goes *through* all those hurtful situations before it reaches the target." So, if you are suffering from any negative experience, know that on the other side of it is joy. And as children illustrate, joy in living is our natural state. Only as we progress into adulthood do we learn to deny that. And those who do not allow themselves to progress through pain, loss, abuse, or death of a loved one, will linger forever in recovery. People in recovery experience little joy because they deny their own personal power and spiritual energy to move on.

During the same workshop, a man sitting in the front row began a droll heckling when I urged people to examine their lives. "So," he asked, "what do you do when a family member has a problem? Ignore him to pursue your own interests?"

"Direct him to a place where he can get help," I replied.

"What do you do when friends call and interrupt you?" he pursued.

"I got an answering machine . . . ask them to call back," I replied. It was the beginning of a day-long set of challenges and tests. Not that he was rude, or even unkind. In fact, he was a charming man who loved giving me the business. I enjoyed poking holes in his theories equally as well. However, at the end of the day, he asked, half-laughingly, "Do you have any friends?" It broke him up when I replied, "No!" Then *everyone* laughed. I followed up by saying that, among thousands of acquaintances, I have a great many people who consider me their friend. Among *them*, however, I consider as friends only those people who are honest, courageous, and true to themselves. His question showed how much most people worry about offending others with the strength of their beliefs—how easily they will dilute their own powers whenever they find their opinions threatening others. Diluting any of your power keeps you from following your dreams. While some people deny their personal powers, others wield it . . . with unhappy consequences for themselves and others.

A young acquaintance bucked family expectation by not attending college. Why go? he reasoned—his family had invested heavily in art and antiques and was about to open a gallery. Since Eric had grown up listening to his parents and grandparents discussing their growing collections, he figured he knew as much—if not more—than most people on the subject. The family gallery opened when Eric was in his early twenties and because he was energetic and knowledgeable, they allowed him to assume the position of executive director. While Eric knows antiques, art, and artists, he *doesn't* know how to appropriately manage the responsibility the family has given him. That's partially because position and its inherent power were given to him, rather than earned. And, while he knows his subject exceptionally well, he has had no training in motivating others, setting a good example, or restraining a natural sense of leadership that appears to be arrogance.

Observation and childhood experience alone rarely qualify anyone to head businesses, companies, or institutions. And when an institution relies upon reciprocity from professors and experts holding graduate degrees in the subject area and training in business management, appropriate attention must be given to their advanced degrees, books, and articles, and years of professional service. Additionally, more than family experience is required in academic standards, acquisition, care, and display. Anyone not having earned those things will find it impossible to be accepted within his or her community. Nor will a family gallery—no matter how wonderful and vast the collection—be accorded the same recognition without a trained CEO. Not surprisingly, both Eric and the collection he represents have been ignored by the powers that be.

How does Eric handle the polite rejection of these highly respected professionals? Imperiously! And he appears to delight in letting them know that his family needs neither their acceptance or affiliation. Watching him continue to demand and denigrate others while posturing over a position that he is not fully qualified to hold, I am concerned that he is heading for a disaster that he is bringing upon himself. People in positions of power—earned or inherited—are eventually held accountable for the way they use it. Because he is not using power responsibly, Eric's use of it at this time becomes self-destructive.

Understanding the Danger That Comes from Ego

The difference between the power of spirit energy and the power of ego is enormous. If you find that using your power is more tiring than inspiring, there is probably still some part of you that wants power for power's sake alone. If you are battling each step of the way to motivate those around you to get things done, re-evaluate not only your group goals, but your own. If you feel a need to always be on the alert, to eliminate or squelch someone who might be better equipped, understand that it is ego—not their qualifications or ambition—that is sapping your power. And if, even in moments of financial, social, political, or bureaucratic victory, you feel obliged to dominate and manipulate those around you, it is your insecurity that is at work. Know that the power you are now wielding is condemning you to a life of mediocrity, and even that will not last forever. Soon, someone else will be "king" or "queen" of your lonely hill. And—for those of you who are dominated by someone who is working from ego—trust your own source of power to change that person. If the person chooses not to change, get away! You cannot allow this type of power to squash yours. Just remember the words beneath a poster of Albert Einstein's powerful visage:

Great spirits have always encountered violent opposition
from mediocre minds.

One way to distinguish if you are empowering or being driven by ego is to ask yourself, Do I usually energize those around me—or put them down?

Learning to Respond Without Ego

Energizing and empowering others comes from ego-less responses that honor the other person's feelings. Ego-less responses—especially questions—illustrate respect for what the other person knows. By honoring and respecting that, the respondent removes potential resistance, and avoids hurting feelings.

Check your automatic responses with those given in the following situations:

1] A child comes home from school full of enthusiasm for what he has learned. "Did you know that it's a myth that George Washington chopped down a cherry tree?" he asks his mother. Ego-less response: "If I knew that, I'd forgotten. Every day you surprise me with how much you learn!"

2] With the youth ball game over, the family is in the car heading home. Although his son's team won, Dad can see many ways the kids can improve. However, until an adult tells them that they need to be better at what they are doing, most kids are pretty much pleased just to have participated. Trouble starts when parents try to point out how the team could improve. But children in youth sports already have coaches; what they need are supportive parents! Ego-less question to boy: "How do you feel about the game?" And, whatever the youngster's statement,

Living from Your Fullest Spirit Power

the ego-less response would be: "It's a real pleasure for me to watch you and your friends play!"

3] Married less than a year, the newlyweds are at odds over an unscheduled purchase made by one or the other. "Did we really need that?" the nonbuyer asks. Ego-less response of buyer: "Why do you ask?" Ego-less response of nonbuyer: "Because we have only so much money, and I want us to have a firm financial base!" If the couple has similar values and are both cognizant of watching spending to reach their common goals, these responses provide an opportunity to discuss earlier agreements. Unexpected purchases can then be negotiated, not fought over.

4] Outraged that a state politician voted against a gun control measure, a woman wrote a letter accusing him of selling out to gun interests. Upon receiving it, he immediately called her to explain precisely how the proposed legislation was flawed. "Why didn't you fix those flaws when the proposition was being written?" she demanded. "Because I'm concentrating my energy on prevention," he replied. "I'm writing legislation for young children." Then he went on to suggest that she help him put on a public forum about gun control. Her ego-less response put direct responsibility onto him—and herself: "A public forum is for those who don't know," she said. "You and I know precisely what needs to be done. So, I don't expect you to *write* gun control legislation, but I expect you to keep abreast of that which is written by others, note your suggested additions or deletions, then send it to me. I'll spend the time it takes to let politicians and the public know what's going on!"

5] A recovering substance abuser demands of a close friend, "Prove to me that my life will be better without cocaine." Ego-less response: "You tell me—how much better would your life be without cocaine?" "Well, I wouldn't have to worry about the police, or overdosing, or running out of money." Ego-less response: "So, with all that energy, money, and time, what's your one wish?" By not passing judgment in the very beginning, the friend not only keeps the substance abuser accountable, he encourages him to plan ahead for a happier future.

6] A woman with an aging parent complains to a friend, "My eighty-six-year-old mother is driving me crazy with her negativity and constant demands. I just don't know what to do." Ego-less response: "How do you want to be treated when you're eighty-six?" Whether the mother has always been negative and demanding, or just recently so, this response shifts the daughter's complaints into another dimension. Suddenly, she can see things from an older person's point of view. Then she can decide how to proceed.

Dream activators always try to respond in creative, loving, intuitive, joyful, expressive, effective, and responsible ways. In this way they become more sure of themselves, direct, dynamic, energetic, and free. That's because dream activators operate from spirit energy and personal power!

Recognizing Ego in Yourself

If you feel that people feel unsafe around you, that you are beset by incompetent employees or co-workers against whom you must protect yourself with secrecy, anger, or fear, know this: before you can achieve—and live peacefully with—a dream, you must rid yourself of that kind of ego-driven power seeking. In fact, make getting rid of it your next dream.

Begin by asking yourself: What are my concerns, and my fears, about being powerful? Write in your journal, or draw pictures of yourself on your art pad of a time that you felt these concerns and fears.

Remember, to rid *ourselves* of fears and insecurities, we need to avoid subduing others for personal gain. Any time that your life work requires you to ignore the needs and feelings of others, you are in danger of subduing them to meet your own needs. Spiritual power, you see, *comes in empowering ourselves and others.*

Denying Power

What if, instead of being ego-ridden, you are a person who *negates* your power. Most people distract themselves from assuming responsibility for themselves by keeping busy with gossip, travel, meetings, or working too much. Others consciously hand over their power to spouses, teachers, attorneys, politicians, doctors, drugs and alcohol, business leaders, and bosses. However, while some people escape their responsibility to and for themselves, millions of others are taking their power back by demanding accountability of those who serve us, and by examining alternatives to long-held practices. By activating their spirit power ordinary people are transforming government, medicine, the law, education, recovery programs, industry, and business. So, it's time to take another look at power; how you claim it, and how you use it.

Ego and Power: The Volatile Two

Are you using your personal power to be in control or in charge? The need to be in control is always about control *over*, rather than sharing power *with*. Rikki, a county employee for many years, had been assuming more and more of the daily responsibilities that her boss was ignoring. Not only was she irritated at having the extra work, she was angry that he took credit for how well she was doing it. The problem here was her ego! Through the following exercise, she identified where the problem lay, which allowed her to move beyond the barrier of ego and start working seriously on her dream.

Using Rikki's situation as an example, substitute one of your own issues and answer the same questions.

1. *What's troubling you? Rikki answered, "I'm doing twice the work for half the money." Your answer?*

2. *What do you want? Rikki: "To prove the boss is taking advantage of me." Your answer?*

3. *Why? Rikki: "To receive acknowledgment for all the work I've done!" Your answer?*

4. *Will that bring you satisfaction? Rikki thinks awhile, then says: "No. I want him to do his own work, too." Your answer?*

5. *Let's take this higher—what do you want for the highest good of both you and your boss? Rikki: "For us each to do our own work." Your answer?*

6. *So what do you need to do? Rikki: "I need to stop doing his work." Your answer?*

7. *Are you going to do that immediately? Rikki: "Well, I'm paying you for this advice, so I'd better get on with it right away!" (And she did!) Can you get on with the changing your attitude about power?*

Having gotten rid of negative thought through positive action, Rikki freed herself to unleash her creative energy. What's equally important is the ego battle going on in Rikki's boss, who—by not doing his own work—set up a work environment that was stifling for her. When Rikki stopped, so did his energy-sapping negative pattern. Now, instead of wasting energy being angry at being used, Rikki is *in charge*.

Writing a New Definition

It's time to move beyond our old concepts. First of all, you must decide that giving them up is what you want to do. Then, clarify what self-established rules you want to live by. The fact is, if you have a great deal invested in living in poor health, you might not want to become well and whole. If you are more comfortable in just getting by each month than in living with the concept of affluence, you're never going to have enough money! How many people have you read about who live on the streets despite having healthy bank accounts? By accepting that poverty is your lot, you will feel poor even if you win a million dollars! The same goes for those who think they aren't smart enough, or pretty enough, that they are victims, or see themselves as always in recovery. If that is what you choose to believe,

Living from Your Fullest Spirit Power

that's what you'll be. If you want to be free of those old concepts, move beyond where you are. And don't get bogged down in recovery. Choose to move beyond recovery to wholeness! It is your choice! By choosing to do so, the following individuals rose above ego and personal limitations to change the lives of their countrymen and women.

In India, Mahatma Ghandi envisioned what would be right for his countrymen and was willing to die for it. Although he chose to oppose the ruling English government in nonviolent ways, his actions placed him in danger every day. But by living what he believed, he moved millions of Indians into a new understanding of their own personal and collective consciousness. And he influenced foreign attitudes toward his countrymen, as well. Ghandi's actions inspired others to use nonviolent ways to change their societies.

Martin Luther King, Jr. awakened white awareness to serious social injustice here in America. John Fitzgerald Kennedy unintentionally lit the spark of overwhelming powerful public response by introducing the concept of a Peace Corps. No one in Washington was prepared for the demand that followed. But that's what happens when an authority empowers others by sharing his or her vision for the future. History records that the people who did this initiated lasting change in whichever century they lived. But these are famous people, you say, what about me? History has also been made by common people who saw a need and met it. You and your ideas are just as valuable as those of the rich and famous!

When retired librarian Maggie Kuhn grew angry over the plight of poor elderly Americans, her objections started a movement that evolved into the Gray Panthers, a group of over-sixty activists who lobbied for new laws and rules governing the rights of older people. When in her mid-twenties, and an unknown reporter, Gloria Steinem objected to the misperceptions then damaging women by exposing the chauvinist mindset in a series of scathing articles, she opened the door to a new level of feminism. The magazine she created some time later, *Ms.,* is still a powerhouse in publishing. And Steinem remains a visible champion of human dignity. Living congruently with the belief that true power is energized by love and concern for others, as well as ourselves, allows us to use the *power of our own spirit.*

Yet, how many people do you know who are willing to raise their hand and say, "I am powerful, and I take full responsibility for that!"? Much of our unwillingness to do that comes from our childhoods. As teenagers, we were trained to be modest—to at least *appear* to apologize for personal power. Captains of sports teams, for instance, traditionally verbalize or show with body language an "aw shucks, it was nothing" attitude toward their accomplishments during awards ceremonies. I'm not encouraging arrogance, but there is nothing wrong with admitting that you've worked very hard to be successful—and that you are pleased and proud that all that hard work paid off. We do the same thing when we encourage our sons and daughters to hide their intelligence. It's better, society says, for them to exhibit good looks, trendy clothes, and popularity. By promoting false modesty and emptiheadedness, we strip teenagers of their personal power. The results can be seen all around us—adult men and women who measure themselves by celebrities and handsome and beautiful models who tell them what brands, fashions, and cars they need to buy to be considered successful.

So we must make a conscious effort to reinstate our native powers of the spirit and individuality. When you accept the naturalness of this combination and use it to accomplish a dream, exuberance replaces boredom. Power of the spirit flourishes in those of us who are so secure in what we know to be fair and true that we don't need to depend upon anyone else's applause or compliance.

Using the power of your spirit is like having access to the ultimate library. When I said this to a group, one person asked, "How do I get a card?" What a great question! And the answer is by clearing away all the obstacles and fully accepting your power so that you can access the power of everything around you. That it has been there all along is not the point. It's like not using the public library that is so conveniently nearby. Suddenly, a road ignored beckons us. There is, for instance, all this talk of an information superhighway. Have you accessed it yet? No, you say, because it is still in theoretical form, and therefore unavailable. Ah ha—not true! If access to this highway has moved from the unconscious to the conscious mind, then it's *real*. So, getting your library card requires nothing but investigation, perseverance, and commitment. Then, the minute information comes on line, you are ready, thereby gaining immediate access to all the communicable intelligence you will ever need. But that access

Living from Your Fullest Spirit Power

is possible only when you make yourself ready for, then activate, your own abilities—or, your own power. Otherwise when the superhighway is available, you'll be lingering at a sign that says Dead End.

Combining Spiritual Power and Personal Power

It is exciting to see dreamers becoming dream activators simply by putting spirit and personal powers into action. Spirit and personal powers differ in that spirit power is the force that is innately ours; we are born with spirit energy. Personal power is based upon what you know, what you learn—in some cases, where you learned it—and who you know. Personal power is that authority that you consciously assume for yourself, and is consciously given to you by others.

Visible Signs of Spirit and Personal Power

To remind myself that even power needs to take a lighthearted turn now and then, I do not hold back when, on a golden day in autumn, I feel the urge to twirl—childlike—in a pile of brightly colored leaves. I don't care that onlookers might not approve. There I whirl, arms outstretched in the sunlight, laughing. By illustrating my love of being alive, I encourage others to cast aside their inhibitions in ways of their own. And some among them might want to illustrate their own passion for *being alive by laughing along—or joining me*. And later on when each of us remembers that golden day, we each smile, remembering the joy of being uninhibited in the love of a beautiful day. Shedding our inhibitions makes us more sure of ourselves, more resilient, more determined than ever to be true to ourselves. That alone makes us more powerful, and when we align our power with our spirit energy, we can fulfill our destiny. The following people have evolved from dreamers to dream activators by tapping into their spirit energy. These are the words they use to describe it:

> Accepting the power and energy of my spirit means
> getting out of my own physical presence and living in my
> God presence, where all my power lives.

To listen within. To pay attention. To act on the guidance given. And to trust that if I am in harmony, within all of life around me is also doing its "right dance" as well.

By welcoming my power, I know myself better each day. This means knowing with clarity and confidence what needs to be done. It allows me to *know me*.

Embracing my own powers means realizing myself for who I truly am, not as others perceive me to be.

How Much Power Do You Want?

How much do you need? How *much* will it require—full-time, occasional, or partial? What choices do the realization of your dream involve? How will you use your power of the spirit to achieve it? How is it different from achieving it through the power of the ego?

Because self-examination is a necessary first step, write to refresh your answers to the important who, what, where, when, and why questions:

- ★ *Why am I here?*
- ★ *What do I want out of life?*
- ★ *What do I want to accomplish or contribute?*
- ★ *Where do I belong?*
- ★ *Where do I want to go?*
- ★ *When should I make my move?*

And is it your power you want to use, or someone else's? All too often, we borrow other people's power, even when there is no longer a need to do so. How many married women continue to ask their husband's permission to go out with female friends long after getting used to socializing without him? How many men are reluctant to make business-related social plans without first consulting with their wives? Is their hesitancy politeness? Consideration? Or is

Living from Your Fullest Spirit Power

it a symbol that the relationship would have evolved faster and *more* had old habits been abandoned? Do we cheat our partners of *their* growth when we treat them at fifty as we did at twenty-six? Is not allowing our relationships to grow a major cause of divorce?

Recently, a retired major league baseball player made some startling remarks during a television interview. When asked about his personal life, he stated that it was no wonder that his earlier marriages had failed. What he had come to realize since retiring, he said, was that management deliberately fostered adolescent behavior in professional ball players. Provided with every material object a person could ever want, public adoration, and outrageous salaries, players had no reason to grow beyond what they had been when first drafted. When did he realize that he was being denied that growth during his career? Not until much later, he said.

Had he believed at the time that he possessed, and used, personal power during those years? Certainly. But, even while he was demanding—and getting—enormous amounts of money, owners and managers had the real power—what he had was the big bat, or the fast ball, or the legs. But how do you know when you are being duped, or manipulated, by bosses, agents, spouses, and friends?

If you aren't learning something new, you are easy prey for those who would rob you of all your powers. Professional sports heroes are prime examples, because they have been led to believe that acquiring a huge amount of money is the answer to their dream. Too many have discovered that it is the answer to only one dream, one that ends all too soon. No matter how outstanding the talent or skill, everyone needs to keep expanding the mind. For high school and college athletes that means attending classes and committing themselves to learning academic subjects—even when coaches and teachers would let them off the hook. For those professional athletes who have not attended college or a training school, do so in the off season. For every young adult in the nation? Take parenting classes. For every adult, no matter the age, become a fully functioning human being by being curious about what you don't know. Then learn!

Will your advancement require leaving friends, and maybe even family members, behind? Sometimes, but, again, as you have already discovered, it's amazing how those around you change when you do. So, while I would hope that marriage partners would grow together, it is not always possible. In the same way we may outgrow organizations and programs that no longer serve us. To be true to ourselves, we must go beyond. So, how much power does a person need? As much as it takes to survive even what appears to be absolute powerlessness. Some former prisoners of war tell of being stripped of everything: clothes, companionship, and light. Some took what seemed to be the easy way and gave up; turned their bodies and minds over to their jailers and let them do whatever they wished. But one prisoner outwitted his captors. Tapping into his own resources, he began planning in intricate detail the house he would build upon release. Day by day throughout his torturous imprisonment, he drew mental pictures of walls, flooring, joists, wiring, and plumbing. By using creative and spiritual powers to survive, he made his imaginary house *real*. And real it is! After being released, that house was built identically to the plans that he'd imagined. Tapping into the power of the spirit is the result of accepting responsibility for personal power.

When I asked myself what accepting all of my spiritual energy and personal power meant to me, I had to start with what was real. And what is real for me are the voices in my head. Sound crazy? Well, the voices I hear, and the insights they give, are very real to me! Those voices correspond with the reality of an idea as opposed to an achieved dream. To illustrate: Does a building project become a reality when it is conceived, when it is committed to a drawing board, when the wood is purchased, when it is built, or when it is painted or varnished? To me, that patio is real the instant it takes shape in the dreamer's mind—just as a book is real, or a painting is real, the moment it is conceived in the author and artist's mind. Having the clarity of mind to *create* it is the hard part; implementing it just takes attention, commitment, desire, and action!

A building project is, of course, a measurable reality. But curiosity is also real, although it cannot be weighed or measured. Television is real, even though most of us do not know the full process of it getting from the studio into our living room. But, while television is real, how about virtual reality? Space travel is real, but quantum leaps are still beyond us. In your lifetime alone, how many

Living from Your Fullest Spirit Power

things that you take for granted have gone from theory to reality? What's next? And when do those new ideas become realities?

During the process of deciding to leave teaching, I had to ask myself some pretty basic questions. Why am I on this planet at this time in history? What was I willing to do to find out? And that is when I had to believe in myself enough to step into the "void." That doesn't mean that I literally stepped off a cliff, although stepping into the unknown seemed like it at the time. But, whether it was a move made from desperation, or faith, it came from my need to move beyond all that was keeping me from serving a larger humanity. Wasn't I doing that when I directed that innovative school? At that moment, yes. But the handwriting was on the wall for the local school board was moving away from what I believed to be best for children. Being a futurist, I wanted to prepare children for the year 2000, not take a step backward. Since I could not live congruently with what was expected, it was necessary for me to move on. This meant creating a new reality for myself. It required that I tap into my personal power, then activate it, for a whole new challenge. So, how much spirit and personal power do you need to accomplish your dream? As much as you need to make the move and get the job done! How do you combine them? By diminishing your need to force others to do your bidding, by removing your ego from decisions and dealings with people, by reacquainting yourself with the innate power you were born with, and by standing back to measure your personal aspirations against the highest good of all involved.

Encourage forward movement by asking, What does accepting my power mean to me? List all those changes occurring in your life because you accepted your own power to work on your dream.

Don't be dismayed if this exercise takes you awhile. When I first sat down and really thought about my power and how it could change my life, I was a bit overwhelmed—mainly because I hadn't really considered that concept before. However, after some serious thought and a few days' breathing room, these are the results I came up with:

1] I will have increasingly clear vision about what my dream entails.

2] I will gain increasing clarity on how I am to pursue it.

3] My income level will allow me to pursue my dream.

4] My work will be congruent with my dream.

Use the following heading to establish a log in which you record each day what changes occur as a result of accepting your fullest power:

All That Has Happened Since Accepting the Power
and Responsibility for Making My Dream Come True

Now, list all those things you've done. You might include:
* *I've established and followed a schedule that suits me.*
* *I'm increasingly in touch with my inner spirit.*
* *This contact is creating an energy all its own.*
* *I've created an office/work/spiritual place just for me.*
* *My heart is lighter from knowing that I am working toward what I love.*
* *I am energized by working with people who believe in me and my dream.*
* *I am socializing with people with dreams of their own.*

Note also how these changes will alter the lives of your family and friends.

Watching the transformation that comes with people realizing and accepting increasing amounts of spirit and personal power is exhilarating. Understanding that the realization of their dream improves the world, they are even more effective than before. That's because they are not only sharing their dream, but their power, with those around them. By sharing power, we enable ourselves to move through the open door and cross the threshold onto our dream path.

Never Again...

Having completed this demanding chapter, you have a better understanding of your power and ego, as well as everyone else's. If you choose, never again will you suffer or abuse either. As you address the following issues, think about character traits you really want to put behind you, although it may seem difficult to do so *right this minute*. By making a commitment to change, however, you begin to rid yourself of negativity and self-depreciating behavior. You begin to recognize what it really means to live from your fullest spirit power.

In gathering information that allows you to stay in your power, list the current headlines and book titles with which you identify.

Describe the times you've recognized your ability to practice using your power effectively and fairly.

List the radio and television programs that are now drawing your attention.

Describe the scenes or list the lines in films that reflect your new view of yourself.

Describe the powerful fictional people with whom your spirit power identifies.

Describe the powerful living people with whom your spirit power identifies.

Living from Your Fullest Spirit Power

Describe the people in your life right now who invite you into the laughter of discovery and thrill you with your loss of limits.

Make the Dream Real... Make It Yours

Ego and worldly and spiritual power are tangible. With conscious use you include them in your life's script. In doing that, you make them real.

You share your power when you say the following...

You share your power when you take the following actions...

Rejoice. By sharing them you make them yours.

CHAPTER 4

Crossing the Threshold

WHAT I WANT MOST IN THE WORLD IS FOR EVERYONE TO BE TRUE to their dreams and work toward whatever it is they want to achieve. That's when everything begins functioning appropriately. That doesn't mean that there aren't challenges or trying days, but—overall—everything works. When it doesn't, we need to pay strict attention. It's our instinct asking us, Are you finished with this part of the dream? Is it time to move on? At this point, you are ready to move through the open door and across its threshold to a place where you further define what it is that you want. Expect, sometimes, to find illumination arriving in the most unexpected ways.

I moved on with my dream because my granddaughter asked the question, "Grandma, am I going to be killed by a nuclear bomb?" Then she made a statement: "Gosh Grandma . . . if you can't end wars, no one can!" There it was—as her grandmother I had a responsibility to make our world safer for my grandchild. It is a responsibility that each of us carries. And if we don't get on with it, there won't be any dreams for anyone! And so I had to take inventory: Why was I on this planet at this time in history? What must I do to fulfill my own destiny so that my granddaughter might fulfill hers? It was up to me, I figured, to go higher. Although this might sound

113

pretentious, or like a slogan for a New Age philosophy, for me, pushing myself to always "go higher" keeps me—and my personal dream—on track. It keeps me moving forward even when I might become lulled into inactivity by a transitory sense of fulfillment. Out of my inner pushing came a further definition of my dream. Because I believe so completely that the salvation of the world depends upon the spiritual, physical, and emotional fulfillment of individuals, I was to begin to do what needed to be done to save the world for my granddaughter—assisting others, as well as myself, to fulfill our dreams.

You must understand that, except to my bemused husband, I made no such public announcement. Yet I set forth right away. With what I know about human nature, motivation, and commitment, I knew that I could accomplish my dream best by becoming a "coach." In other people's success would be my own. Aligning our fulfilled energies, we would extend our inner peace to those around us. You know the rest . . . by sharing our peace, eventually the entire world becomes a better place for all of humanity.

Moving Ahead—A Personal Experience

Looking back on the last twelve years, my journey has been extraordinary. In my rear view mirror, I can see that in going from teaching youngsters to coaching adults, I simply enlarged my classroom. However, that's hindsight. Setting off on that first day, I had only the most rudimentary chart showing me where I was—or indicating my destination. In between the two lay a forest of unfamiliar roads, paths, and byways. I think I took them all, and what I learned is that there are no dead ends. There are detours, however . . . and surface roads instead of freeways. However, I found some of those postponed routes to be blessings in disguise, for down some of the most unlikely paths I found unexpected support and guidance. So, through discovery and loss, setbacks, and joys, I've accumulated people and friendships and victories that I might never have known had I not slowed down long enough to take a more in-depth look at where I was, how I'd gotten there, and the determination of the route by which I would finally arrive.

Remaining in the Wishing Stage Gets You Nowhere—and Nothing

My mother had two dreams: to own a fur coat, and to take a train trip to the East Coast. She got neither. Sure, rationing during World War II put a serious crimp in travel and the availability of luxury items, but that war ended when she was forty-five. And before the next one began, the economy was doing very well in providing her with ample amounts of money. So, it wasn't war, and it wasn't money that kept my mother from her dreams. It was remaining at the wishing stage—and a reliance upon others to deliver her dreams to her doorstep—that kept that fur coat and trip east "pie in the sky" dreams. Don't do that! Cross that threshold by taking charge of your dream!

Assuming Total Responsibility

A mid-thirties client was the pleasant young wife of a successful man. On the surface, it appeared that she had everything a person could want. Yet, she said she'd joined my Live Your Dream workshop to get her life in order. Her dream? To provide a stable life for herself and her children. But, when other group members discussed *living* their dreams, she said that she couldn't ". . . until I get my laundry done!" *Laundry? Laundry* was stopping her?

Instinctively, Myra knew that the current state of her house reflected the disorder in her entire life. So, she had done the only thing that seemed sensible to her: she signed up for my workshop to learn *how* to restore order and find purpose in her life. With a clean and tidy house, she figured that her relationship with her family would improve and she could get on with her dream. Finally, she thought, she would be happy.

Realizing from working with a group that she needed more coaching at this stage in her life, Myra asked for a coaching session in her home. It wasn't until I got there that I realized just how out of control things were. Rooms were in complete disarray. The laundry, clean and dirty side-by-side, took up an entire room and rose nearly to the ceiling.

While Myra was quick to accept responsibility for having created the chaos, she wasn't certain until my visit that she could take charge. Except, this was a woman who had never *heard* the term "time management." Even making

Crossing the Threshold

a list of what needed to be done seemed to be beyond her. Together, we discussed how we might get her home ready for a party. As she described her steps, I wrote them down. Then, we designed an efficient timetable for washing, drying, folding, and ironing clothes. The household budget allowed her to hire a cleaning service to come in each week to care for the rest of the house. In a rather short period of time, physical order was restored.

Myra then turned her attention to the yard, hiring a gardener to shape up the flower beds and keep the grass mowed, and a handyman to finish uncompleted projects. With everything in good order, it was time for Myra to get on with the next step toward providing a stable environment for her children. But, with hours each day suddenly available, Myra had time to realize that it wasn't just an untidy house and yard that had been making her unhappy. It was her husband's frequent absences, her children's constant complaints, and the never-ending demands of her alcoholic parents and adult siblings. So Myra had to step aside and take a good look at what she had not wanted to see before. Only then could she begin to create another—better—reality.

As I've said, before we can change those around us—and the world—we must first change ourselves. And Myra did. Over the next two years she reviewed her childhood. Finding that, like many children of alcoholic parents, she'd carried the uncertainties of childhood into her adult life. Because she *never* knew what was expected of her, she rarely finished anything she started. Never having received coherent directions, she was incapable of giving them. So, although her home was functioning much more smoothly, her children could still not expect meals to be served on time, if at all. It was the same in the homes of her parents, brothers, and sisters. On top of that, Myra had to accept another fact: her husband was an alcoholic, too. If there was to be a stable environment, she alone had to provide it. Which meant that she needed to find out what was "normal." Reading self-help and child development books I assigned, she then joined an Adult Children of Alcoholics support group. Working with school staff, she learned how to enforce normal disciplinary measures at home. By letting her children know that she was in charge, she let them know that it was safe for them to be children. In other words, by becoming stable herself, Myra was living congruently with what she wanted in her life.

This has not been a quick journey. It took five years, a degree in business, detaching from her dysfunctional family, and a divorce for Myra to establish a well-functioning life. And it hasn't been easy, either. A romance—with another alcoholic—showed her how vigilant she must be not to repeat earlier mistakes. But what she's won is the respect and love of her children, *self*-respect, and wonderful reasons to get up in the morning. Was I disappointed when she had the romance with another alcoholic? Yes! But even dream coaches have lessons—Myra has been in my life to illustrate that *I could just as easily be pulled away from my own dream!* You see, I cannot work with anyone who is not living congruently with what he or she says he or she wants to be, do, and have. Because my dream is to change the world by helping individuals attain their dreams, I had to step aside from Myra until she went back to taking the steps required to improve her life, and her children's. With her alcoholic love interest out of the picture, she is ready to continue and I am working with her again. Idle wishes are okay, just not for dream activators. Harmful old habits and fear of change aren't for dream activators, either. Taking charge and persistence is!

Persisting Allows for Small Successes Along the Way

Rick is a perfect example of someone who, by living congruently with his dream, has enjoyed many successes along his way. At the age of twenty-five, Rick was unsure of what he wanted to do after college. What he liked to do most, he confessed, was play. At my suggestion, he listed all the things he considered "play." Then he listed the talents and abilities he possessed, along with all the skills he'd acquired from various jobs he'd held. Proudly, he rattled them off: he could read, write, talk, deliver papers, build houses, cook, wait tables, clean houses, fix any kind of plumbing, baby-sit, compete as a cross-country runner, play tennis, surf, wind surf, roller blade, and ski. What this list suggested was that he was well equipped not only to play himself, but to teach others to play, as well. While still thinking this over, Rick had a fateful encounter at the beach.

Crossing the Threshold

With his surfboard under his arm, Rick happened by a staged modeling "shoot." When it was over, he strolled over to the photographer and asked how a person got started in the modeling business. Automatically, the photographer told him to get a portfolio of good head and action shots, then find an agency to represent him. Asking for the man's card, Rick asked when he could call for an appointment. Barely looking up from what he was doing, the photographer said, "tomorrow." But the next morning when Rick called, the photographer was surprised. In his experience, he said, people rarely followed through on suggestions given. But Rick did. Having opened the door on a potential dream, he began the process of crossing the threshold.

There followed years of reading, training, and traveling as Rick circled the world as a professional model. And, as happens when people are in total alignment with their natural talents and skills, new opportunities, new ideas . . . even new thresholds . . . appeared. What Rick discovered was that the part of modeling that he enjoyed most was the performing part. Once again, he began reading up on what it took to be an actor. In the months that followed, he studied acting techniques used by actors in plays and films— and he began concentrating on getting the modeling jobs that involved performing. What Rick had discovered is that he could support himself in several ways—and in ways congruent with the life he wanted to lead—but not consistently. However, as Rick says, "If playing for a living was easy, everybody would be doing it!"

So, Rick, instead of stopping, getting too comfortable or complacent, took what he'd learned and moved on.

Rick's one dream was becoming clearer. Simply put, he wanted to live each moment of his life as fully as he could. He wanted to express himself congruently with who he was and what he knew. So, between assignments, Rick supported himself by waiting tables, got married, continued modeling and studying acting. Then, in the mid-1980s, he decided that he needed a firmer financial base. Returning to his home town he became the engaging managing partner in a very busy beach-city bistro. For Rick, running a business allows him to be who he is: friendly, compassionate, and helpful to patrons and staff alike. Being his own boss also allows him to continue modeling, and performing in local, semi-professional theater. Is that congruent? Is it persistent? Well, his brother recently commented, "Rick you're the only person I know that lives life as if it were a vacation!"

Going Beyond Initial Accomplishments

Speaking of small and large successes, sometimes what we consider a small success becomes a larger success for others. A former newspaper editor and his wife moved out of state upon retiring, intent upon hiding from the world. To keep himself occupied, Jim planted a vegetable garden. Successful beyond his wildest dreams, he was faced in a few months with a mountain of fresh produce. So, this man who sought time away from the formal service organizations of his professional past has returned to service—but in his way: three times a week he packs boxes of fresh tomatoes, green peppers, different varieties of lettuce, carrots, and cabbages into his truck and drives fifty miles into the nearest large city where he donates it to a refuge for battered women and children. That wasn't what he planned; what he'd looked for was something to keep him physically and mentally alert. Does he celebrate his garden? You bet he does—every day of the week. Is he fully aware of the difference his contribution is making? Maybe not, and that isn't necessary. What *is* necessary, however, is that he activated his dream. Once activated, the dream expanded to meet the needs of others. Your dream, too, must involve your health, work, spiritual development, relationships, finances, and creative expression. By becoming all that you can be right now, you are able to become and do what you want tomorrow! And what you may find is that your dream is benefiting not only you, but others as well.

That is certainly true for my fifty-something client Francine, who thought it was time that she relax and enjoy her husband of thirty years. Unfortunately, he decided at the same time to leave her and start life anew with a younger woman. Destroyed, Francine took five years to even think about healing the wounds. She started that process when she moved away from her old hurts and pains. Settling in Southern California, she met me through a local business owner. Unhappy enough to make an appointment, Francine enrolled in one of my journaling workshops to rediscover how she could recover her confidence and joy in living.

Through journaling and her commitment to creating a new life, Francine was inspired to seek out advisors to assist her. By consulting with a nutritionist she revised her health habits. After contracting with an image consultant she began making outward changes that reflected what was going on inside. Changing her diet, updating her clothes and hair style, and learning how to apply fashionable make-up, Francine was soon looking and feeling like a new person. It was at this point that she first saw reason for a little joy. And she did, with a small group of friends. Not stopping there, she continued attending lectures, reading, using advisors when she felt it necessary, and journaling to continue the growth she'd begun. Some of the advisors she hired were an investment counselor, a real estate adviser, and a broker to manage property she'd inherited. With the completion of each step, she celebrated with an ever-expanding group of friends. Today, Francine is an exceptionally happy woman who regularly contributes to local hospitals and the arts. She continues to celebrate each and every day. But she's not the only one—a *great many* people celebrate Francine's dream!

Taking Time to THINK!

The people in the foregoing stories gave a lot of thought to who they were, where they'd come from, and where they were going. When was the last time you took time to examine what is going on in *your* life? In your head? In your heart? For that matter, when did you last spend an entire day by yourself? And when did you last spend an entire day *just thinking*?

All too few of us make time to just *be*—even when we know how important it is to sit in the silence and listen to what we are trying to tell ourselves. Because we have integrated earlier dreams into our day-to-day lives, we expect more of ourselves than ever before. That too often means that we are busier than ever and have not stopped to take more than fifteen minutes or half an hour to reflect. Yet, if we are to continue activating our dream by crossing the threshold into new experiences—we need to dedicate more thinking time *each day* to assess where we are! By not doing so, we may be missing something.

Take the next half an hour to begin thinking about where you want to be in the next six months. Are you ahead of schedule? Or, is it time to move on?

Taking MORE Time to Think and Dream

Answers to questions like the above may require even more time, possibly an entire day of contemplation. That means developing a new habit of regularly scheduling hours away from the phone, friends, family, associates, and regular activities. It means retreating to a place of tranquillity—a drive in the country, a visit to an art gallery, museum, forest, monastery, desert, seashore, library, or out to the middle of a cornfield—wherever you find serenity.

Begin to arrange your schedule so that you can spend one, two, or three days in that peaceful place. And when you go, be sure to take your journal, your art pad, any art supplies, to capture your thoughts and feelings.

Dreaming Dreams: Yours, and Others

While you were thinking, did you ask yourself if the dream you are working on is yours, or someone else's? This is a question I'm often asked. You do know intuitively if you are following your own dream, or supporting someone else's! And, you may be realizing that, to reach your own dream, you may *have* to work on someone else's first. A good example might be, if you want to be mayor of your city, you may need to work to support the current mayor to learn the ropes and build up a constituency. It is vital that you really *do* support the current mayor, of course. To support someone you do not respect is, of course, living incongruently with your own highest standards. On the other hand, you might enter politics to discover if this *is* *really* your dream by supporting that mayor *without* having a plan to succeed him or her. Is there a hard-and-fast rule by which you always know what your next step is going to be? No. Not always. Each of us is different, and so

Crossing the Threshold

are our individual circumstances. But whenever you feel alive when working on a dream—yours or someone else's—you are at that moment traveling the right path. Just be aware that when your personal passion is not aroused, or begins to fade, the dream you are giving your energy to may not be related to your own.

Another way of knowing if you are working on your dream, is to ask yourself if you are operating in your own personal and spirit power, or in someone else's. If you are subordinating your powers to someone else—or to a company, organization, or movement—you will always feel that something is missing. It may appear as a sense of loss, recurring illnesses, stress, or vague unhappiness. This happens all too often in the workplace, where having an income may be taking precedence over what we *really* want to do. Frequently, we started out enthusiastically learning all that we could learn on that job. But years of repetition, or maturation and personal growth taking us beyond confines of our workplace, has led to our emotional and creative burn-out.

Mothers, fathers, caregivers, even grandparents, too often minimize personal dreams to give time and effort to dependents. While "living for others" sounds terribly noble . . . it doesn't have to be a permanent extension of being a provider. Raising healthy, happy children to responsible adulthood is, indeed, a virtuous accomplishment . . . as long as it isn't a substitute for getting on with personal development. Not to do so makes living for others cowardly instead of righteous. Just as detrimental are the cases where children are expected to live a parent's dream. The results of that are to be seen in the acting out of the offspring of the rich, influential, and powerful—even as adults. Robbed of their right to have a dream of their own, choose, and experience personal fulfillment, they are without purpose. Everyone must be allowed to live in his or her own power. Everyone needs his or her own dreams . . . his or her own personal spotlight.

For some, destiny *does* lay in carrying on a dream for someone else. Or supporting someone else's dream. Natalya Solzhenitsyn, wife of Russian author Alexander Solzhenitsyn, is a fine example of someone who understands direction in the role she takes in another person's life. When asked by a television interviewer how she viewed herself in relationship to her famous husband, she replied that she loved work. It appears that *her* work is making sure that he receives the support to get *his* work done.

Graphing Your Way to Knowing Whose Dream You're Pursuing

Having elected to cross the threshold to a dream, let's measure the time and commitment you are spending on its fulfillment. Keep track of the minutes and hours—in fifteen-minute segments—you spend thinking about, or actively pursuing, a dream for a twenty-four-hour period. I recommend doing this exercise for at least a month, or until you know that you are in your own personal dream . . . or someone else's.

Select one color to represent time spent thinking and/or time spent actively pursuing the dream you're working on. Begin charting upon awakening each day, and end when you go to bed.

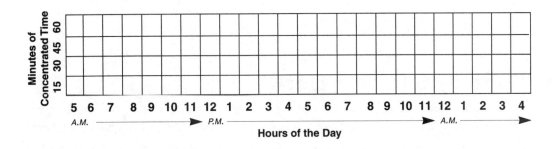

Your graphing shows you how much time and energy you are expending on a dream. What did you feel whenever you logged that time onto the graph? Elated? Thrilled? Energized? Then you are living your dream!

Or, did you avoid logging the time on the graph? Did you feel discomfort, or resistance? Did you get physical symptoms of illness? If so, you are probably living up to someone else's expectations, or dreams.

For those of you after your own personal dream, there are more questions: Do you need to make changes in the way you direct and use your time? Perhaps what you need is to reduce/eliminate activities and practices that conflict with the mental image you have of living your dream. As you rid your life of non-dream-related duties, the closer you come to making your one dream a reality.

Crossing the Threshold

Replacing the Old with the New

If you're stuck on knowing what to replace the non-dream activities with, consider introducing yourself to new groups of people or changing jobs. How about going back to school, losing fifteen pounds, gaining fifteen pounds, studying metaphysics, traveling, coloring your hair, stopping coloring your hair, going back to playing the clarinet, being the only forty-five-year-old man in a beginning ballet class, auditioning for a part in community theater, volunteering for a worthy cause or charity, becoming a foster parent or big brother/sister, running for office, bicycling across the country, taking up weaving, joining the Peace Corps or the urban youth service, Americorps. Whatever, *stretch* your brain, your emotions, and your body. By investigating new practices related to your dream, your interests grow. In stimulating your interests to things beyond what you've been doing, you move forward. In moving forward, you meet new people, learn new skills, enjoy life more. All this brings you closer to your dream.

Running into Your Fears

"But," you object, "what if I choose the wrong thing? I haven't got time for mistakes." Let me tell you about a marketing specialist who came to me. She said that she knew exactly what she wanted, and how fast she wanted to get it. She was a bright, aggressive young woman who had already achieved considerable success and was eager to take the next step to a new dream.

During our first meeting, she established what it was she wanted, and her timeline for meeting those goals. Together, we drew up a list of what needed to be done. She rapidly completed the first week's tasks and assignments. The second week, she did most of them. The third week—well, the third week she didn't do anything. As her coach, it was *my* responsibility to find out why. Here were my questions, and her answers.

1] Were the tasks or assignments she'd picked too difficult? No!

2] Had she failed at anything she'd undertaken so far? No!

3] Then what was holding her back? After a long, contemplative pause, she confessed, "It's going too fast!"

Mind you—here was a heavy-duty achiever; she'd accomplished many of her earlier dreams in record time. And this was *her* schedule we were meeting. She had come to realize that she was afraid that she hadn't had the appropriate training to be as powerful as she wanted to be. Never, had she pressed herself to stretch this far or fast before. Not only that, up to this point she'd had models to imitate and other people's dreams to follow. While her dream was to go farther than anyone else had gone, *pioneering* a role required that she step into a mental and emotional void. What she'd have to do is create new guidelines. Even scarier, it might mean admitting to others that she didn't have all the questions, much less the answers. Overwhelmed by these realities, she pulled back. Right now, she thinks she's hit a dead end. In reality, she's only taken a detour. That is all right—as long as comfort doesn't permanently keep her there.

Remember Linda, the New York editor who moved to California to start her own free-lance editing business? She says that, with all of her big-city-name publisher experience, she remained in her job for nearly three years past the time she wanted to leave. Why? Fear! Fear that her New York associates would think she was leaving because she couldn't "cut" it, anymore. Fear that, maybe, she wouldn't make it. How could she explain that to family and friends? Now that she's overcome all that, she's looking toward another dream—establishing a home for battered women for her part of the city. And, guess what? The same old fears are surfacing again. What will people think? Will she compromise her income to the point she has to back out? Funny how old fears crop up, even when we're at our most successful in life. This is why it's so important to keep seeking clarity about what you want. The soul-searching you do will lead you to uncover your fears and hesitations and meet them face to face.

Getting Clarity through Self-inventory

The average person requires some professional help somewhere along the line. However, before you rush out and buy training videos, enroll in college, get a bank loan, engage a financial advisor, a broker, or investment counselor, there are decisions that only *you* can make. After determining precisely what your dream is going to require, you might find that you require a career counselor or a professional recruiter. For someone wanting to be a physician, it may not only mean bank loans, but the support of an entire community to whom the future doctor pledges the first five years of his or her medical career. For a person wanting to be a model, dental work might be required, along with acting classes, photographer fees, and an agent. So, whatever it is you want, or want to be, observe everything you can about people who are already there. As Socrates wrote, "The unexamined life is not worth living." So, before you determine what type of assistance you might want, let's examine more specifically what else you may need to advance your dream.

Mark those areas that you feel may provide you with some of the information you require to inform and expand you:

❑ Motivational tapes

❑ Meditation tapes

❑ Books/libraries

❑ Self-inventory

❑ College degree

❑ Mentor

❑ Gardener

❑ Hypnotherapist

❑ Massage therapist

❑ Image consultant

❑ Marketing firm

❑ Secretarial services

❑ Financial advisor

❑ Physician

❑ Nutritionist

❑ Party consultant

❑ Attorney

❑ Travel advisor

❑ Literary agent

❑ Video feedback consultant

❑ Publicist

❑ Postgraduate education

❑ Child care/nanny

❑ Voice coach

❑ Speech coach

❑ Dream coach

❑ Personal growth consultant

❑ Housekeeper/cleaning service

❑ Vocational education/training

❑ Counselor/therapist/psychiatrist

❑ Exercise coach/consultant/trainer

❑ Movies, plays, musical or artistic events

❑ New or expanded empowerment group

❑ On-the-job-experience/apprenticeship

❑ Certification for _____

SPECIAL INTEREST CLASSES/WORKSHOPS:

❑ acting/drama

❑ assertiveness

❑ parenting

❑ communication skills

❑ personal growth

❑ financial planning

❑ journaling

❑ musical instruction

❑ painting/drawing/sculpture

❑ classes on play, fun, humor

❑ dance/movement/aerobics

❑ other

Aligning with What You Want and Need

Having crossed the threshold, you may now be entering unknown territory. Depending upon what you checked on the list, you may need one or more guides. As the marketing specialist in the section on fear discovered, going it alone can be scary, maybe even overwhelming! To put those concerns in their appropriate perspective, dream activators know that help is everywhere. This calls for another step aside because you, yourself, don't need to know everything. You can arrange for, or hire, what you need to get to where you want to be. Drawing up a plan of action is what comes next.

*Get out your art pad, once again. Using the people and things you've checked, start to develop your plan of action by writing them down in the order that you intend to use them. Then, as this listing is necessarily linear, send yourself beyond its sequential thinking by doing the kinds of graphics you might do on a computer: if you've listed motivational tapes, then draw or paste on a picture of a video or audio tape. Illustrating each of your steps stirs the subconscious and awakens your spirit power. By doing this, you are aligning with your dream. So, sign up for the classes you've identified with, interview the professionals you're going to need . . . and get going! Then, taking another look at your list, note who and what **isn't** on it.*

Anyone and/or anything that is not on the list but is in your life, doesn't belong there. For me, right now that means that I cannot watch television—not even great television. Watching it changes my focus. Watching television disempowers my dream.

Telling Your Own Truth to Further Empower Your Dream

Very, very few people tell themselves the whole truth, although each of us has his or her own truth. Primarily this is communicated through language, both speech and body. Remember back when you were nine or ten, before your parents squished the demanding brat out of you? Back then you knew what you wanted to do and say! And while it was appropriate for your parents to make you acceptable for society, they also harnessed parts of you including what you said that—as adults—are perfectly appropriate for you to say.

So go back and observe that uncurbed child that you were. Ask yourself what you would have thought about your dream back then. How would you have described your wishes? What would you have demanded to make it come true? Then, editing those feelings and words so that you aren't saying what you think other people want to hear, or limiting them to what you think is or is not possible, express what you think about your dream in writing as honestly and purely as you would have when you were ten years old.

Dream activators learn not to allow false politeness to remain a part of their lives. That means that, once you become a person who is committed to a task, you can no longer put up with behaviors—your own or anyone else's—that are incompatible with what you are trying to become or achieve. At the same time, there is no room to direct blame, shame, or guilt at yourself or others. From the moment you assume absolute responsibility for the realization of your dream, you can blame no one else for difficulties encountered. Accept problems and know the freedom that comes from knowing what you want—the emancipation that comes from working toward getting it. So, once you've uncovered that dream, let others know of your intent. When you align with what you want, your dream should be a secret no more.

Does this mean you should be rude, or cruel, or thoughtless? Absolutely not! Never! Certainly, being diplomatic aids others in understanding what your newly announced needs and ideas are; even better, when you live your dream, you free those around you to express themselves and live their dreams, too. By coming out and saying what you are thinking, you create opportunities for others to do the same. By following your example, they may re-examine their lives and grow, too. So, get into the habit of allowing yourself to *feel* everything! Think everything. Avoid nothing, and when you see and hear *your* truth, align with it and speak it freely. Liberated from everything holding you back, you can get on with the work of manifesting your dream. So, experience the moment: if you are happy—*be* happy! If you are sad—know that *it is all right* to be sad. If you feel passionate about something, experience the fervor and express it appropriately. If you want and need support, reach out and find it through empowering people and experiences.

Placing Yourself in Empowering Environments

My friend John loves Dixieland music. For years, he attended local sessions and three-and-a-half-week-long band concerts throughout the state. And what he really wanted was to be *personally involved*. Unfortunately, he could neither sing or play an instrument well enough to be considered band member material. John found a way to become involved anyway—by volunteering to man the tape sales booth several hours each day during local events. Is he satisfied? Not completely, because what he'd really like to do is to solo on the trumpet in public. Because he's no better than most former high school trumpeters, he only accompanies taped tunes at home—with the doors closed. John finds that even his clandestine bugling is more fun now, because most of the Dixieland amateurs and professionals he works with recognize the contribution he makes in selling their tapes. Their thanks give him cause to celebrate his decision to join them and claim them as part of his empowerment team. And they take time to encourage him, too. So if you love—and have little talent for—barbershop singing, opera, fine art, or writing, find a way to align with those who do: sell or take tickets, usher, become a docent, collect information for a newsletter, be on a telephone committee, or help in money-raising efforts to support your favorite group. It takes more than outstanding talent to keep the arts alive so get moving in the right direction with the right people. Taking action empowers you . . . and your dream.

In the same way, if your dream is to become a thoracic surgeon and you have yet to start medical school, volunteer at a hospital where you will associate with people already working in your field. If, for another example, you wish to use your art training to become a full-time book illustrator, attend one of the hundreds of writers/illustrators conferences offered through college and university extensions to learn who in the publishing business can give you some direction. If owning your own business is your dream, make an appointment with the Small Business Association and get a mentor. Attend local Chamber of Commerce meetings. Join, and become active in, local, state, and/or national service groups. Whatever your interest, at least one magazine will be in publication to meet your needs. Subscribe! By activating even the first stages of your dream, you take control of your future. And the people you associate with become an *empowerment team*. They don't have to know one another, or meet formally. However, each of these people consciously takes responsibility to listen to you, encourage you, and/or make appropriate recommendations.

Using Your Empowerment Team

While having a group of special people in an empowerment team is always an ongoing desire, most people find groups frequently provide more support than direction. Although they may no longer be able to contribute what you need as you move on, members of your groups are tremendous co-celebrants. My friend Virginia has the voice of an angel. At the urging of a neighbor, she tried out for a prestigious local choir. She did, and against tremendous competition, won a place in the soprano section. The next few months were spent preparing for a city-wide concert, but when Virginia tried to get her family to attend the concert, everyone was too busy. When she called the neighbor who'd started the whole thing, the neighbor had previous plans. My friend sang that night in the choir, but she dropped out the following week. Why, when she enjoyed it so? Because part of her enjoyment lay in having her family and friends enjoy her triumph *with* her. What Virginia needed was an empowerment team *outside* of her family and immediate friends. Without anyone to appreciate her and the music she helped create, it wasn't worth it to continue. Is the rest of her life fulfilling? you may ask. As you might suspect, it's full of compromises. And the voice that could have lifted her out of compromise has been silenced, a voice that might have comforted some, entertained many, and inspired still others to pursue their own dreams. Now the world has lost that voice. When a dream dies, everyone loses.

Cheering and Sabotaging Sometimes Come in the Form of Support

On the other hand, be forewarned that false cheering can be just as destructive as no cheering at all. How many times have you, or people you know, been "comforted" after a setback with, "That's all right, Honey. I still love you!"? Would that person still have loved "Honey" if he or she had succeeded?

That type of statement is like the dozen roses that are supposed to make up for cruel words or thoughtless behavior. Those posies are nothing but betrayal's mask—yet false patronage like that can be very seductive. Enough of it and a person begins substituting material gain for real support—for awhile. Eventually, the thrill of the new acquisition wears off and the recipient feels a return of emptiness. So make certain that you are truly supported by those around you. What would a supportive spouse say to a partner who failed? "It's only a setback" or "I have every faith in your ability to win next time." A *really* supportive person says, "How about if I take over some of the household chores to give you some extra time to work?" or "Let's hire someone to mow the lawn and weed the garden so you are free to do research, or invent, or design, or build a boat." That's real empowerment—know the difference!

Identifying the Characteristics That Empower You

Now that you know better what you might be needing, I want you to be clear about the characteristics you want in those on your empowerment team, and every aspect of your life. Realization of your dream depends a great deal on the personality and habits of those who assist and surround you.

Check those teaching characteristics in your empowerment team members that you believe are essential to your learning. After all, what could be more important than having the right guidance?

❑ Single	❑ Creative	❑ Intelligent	❑ Physically attractive
❑ Male	❑ Happy	❑ Perceptive	❑ Nurturing
❑ Female	❑ Optimistic	❑ Consciousness	❑ Adventuresome
❑ Young or old	❑ Powerful	❑ Disciplined	❑ Dependable
❑ Humorous	❑ Courageous	❑ Visionary	❑ Religious
❑ Curious	❑ Stimulating	❑ Tidy/orderly	❑ Spiritual
❑ Generous	❑ Honest	❑ Accurate	❑ Psychic
❑ Married	❑ Congruent	❑ Organized	❑ Personally successful
❑ Professionally successful		❑ Dedicated to helping me make my dream come true	

Crossing the Threshold

Talking About Your Dream Gives It a Power of Its Own

By now, you probably have the confidence to enjoy living in the reality you've created by crossing the threshold of your dream toward your life's work. Talking to your friends, family members, and colleagues about your dream is part of what has become natural.

The following questions are wonderful to include in your daily thinking, as well as in any and all conversation.

1] What is your one dream?

2] What did you do today to realize your dream?

3] What action steps are you taking to reach your dream?

4] What did accepting your power mean to you at this stage of your life?

5] How did accepting your power enhance someone else's life?

6] What smaller dreams are you realizing?

7] How did you celebrate each one of them?

8] Have you identified any additional challenges and opportunities?

9] What is your plan for managing them?

10] Are you finding/needing a coach/advisor/mentor?

11] How will using a coach/advisor/mentor further empower you?

12] What steps are you taking to further empower your dream?

13] What changes are you experiencing?

14] What parts of your life are congruent with your dream? Which are not?

15] Are you jumping eagerly out of bed each morning?

16] What new people are in your life? Describe them.

17] What new things are in your life?

18] What did you do today that made your heart sing and your spirit soar?

19] Are you finding yourself thinking and acting more creatively, now?

20] How has moving into your dream changed your outlook on life?

21] How has moving your dream changed your outlook on *you*?

As you get together with empowerment group members, friends, and family, it might be inspiring for all of you to ask these questions of each other. As time goes on, you will undoubtedly add questions to the twenty-one suggested. Talking about your dream empowers you . . . and others, too! Especially when you must combat the biases and setbacks of non-dreamers who proudly believe that they, and they alone, live in the real world.

Never Again . . .

Having crossed the threshold, never again will you perceive limiting people or surroundings as restrictive. Nor will you remain for long in an environment that chafes or binds. As you address the following issues, think about what "crossing the threshold" really means to you, and how you notice it taking form in your own world. Write about how crossing the threshold allows you to more fully embrace your dream.

List the headlines and titles you suddenly noticed that would have missed your attention before.

List the radio and television programs congruent with your dream that you are scheduling into your weekly activities.

Describe the "crossing the threshold" scenes in movies that parallel the steps you are taking.

Describe the people who have supported you during the testing of your dedication to achieving your dream.

Describe the people who cheer you on and help you celebrate who you are and where you are going.

Make the Dream Real ... Make it Yours

You are fully aware of the current thresholds to be encountered and crossed. You step over them with awareness, but no fear. Add courage to your script.

Talk about how adding courage to your life strengthens and empowers your dream.

Rejoice. You know that from this point on, all thresholds will be congruent with achieving your one dream.

CHAPTER 5

Living Your Dream in the Real World

DESPITE BEING IN CLOSER TOUCH WITH OUR INNER AND OUTER selves, we may still encounter old obstacles with new veneers and even some fresh challenges as we progress. So, I want to address the tough times that are bound to occur.

First, of course, you have to recognize tough times when they are upon you. You are probably asking, "How can I miss a setback, a change, a delay, or a problem?" Amazingly enough, sometimes it's easy. By way of explanation—and warning—I must tell you that one of the most paralyzing times can come with getting too comfortable. To illustrate: if you haven't completed your dream but things are going along so well that you just want to sit in the sun and enjoy yourself . . . chances are that you're facing one of your biggest challenges and you don't even know it!

What's wrong with a little rest and relaxation? Nothing, as long as resting and relaxing is directly related to your dream—just don't lull yourself into thinking that a momentary rest is fulfillment. So, whenever your life becomes too comfortable, take a closer look at yourself—it's extremely difficult to move beyond contentment. Therefore, any time that you are feeling really satisfied, check to make sure your forward movement hasn't come to a standstill. If it has, sitting in the sun isn't bringing you any closer to your dream.

To get back on track, know that, if you are to reach your dream, even vacations or laying around times should be directly related to it. For instance, if sitting in the sun is part, or all, of your dream and that's what you are doing—*celebrate*! If your dream is to write a book and you take a month off to think about it—*celebrate*! However, if your dream is to build a new winter resort, it doesn't further you to take a summer vacation in Florida. Unless, of course, that's where you are finding investment capital or something else correlated to getting your resort on line. Dream activators enjoy a lot of things on the way to fulfilling their dreams, and they never allow themselves to lose sight of what they are doing on the way to where they are going. So beware of comfort!

Standing Aside

To have a better understanding of your comfort level, practice viewing your present situation as an outsider. In that way, you get a clearer view of what's really going on. What you want to identify is:

* How many times a week are you thinking and acting as if you are already in the next stage of your dream?

* How often each day are you assuming you are living according to that dream?

* How many times an hour are you aware of—and living according to—your dream?

Actively living your dream by regularly thinking, behaving, and sounding as if it has already been accomplished allows you to be what you are seeking to become. While everything in your life is neither finished or completely resolved, it's getting better. But, don't get distracted by that. Lingering in "getting better" can easily become *comfortable.*

Stepping aside is an ongoing process; there will always be something to detach yourself from; always something more to examine, to learn, to experience. Simply attaining the years needed to be classified as an adult doesn't automatically provide you with complete knowing, understanding, insight, happiness, or the skills and methods toward achieving those things. It takes conscious diligence to become an actualized dream activator.

Take time to write answers to the following questions in your journal.

★ *What in my life do I want and need to detach from?*

★ *What do I want to replace it with?*

★ *What is my plan, and when do intend to start?*

★ *Can anyone in my empowerment team advise me? Who?*

These are questions you will be asking yourself throughout your life, so my advice to you is to answer the above questions whenever you face a potential need to step aside. And, you will benefit if, at those times, you review what previous answers you gave . . . they may continue to give you direction.

Slipping Back into Old Habits, Beliefs, Behaviors, and Patterns

Every day, remind yourself that your dream belongs to you. Write that on your mirror! No one else can own it, and no one can take it away—unless you let them do so. By relaxing her vigilance, my neighbor Carly knew that her entire family was jeopardizing her dream.

Several years before, Carly had realized that if she was ever to have a life of her own she would have to break away from her dominating parents and incessantly complaining, needy brothers and sisters. So Carly moved fifteen hundred miles away, established herself professionally in a new city, met a wonderful man with similar goals, and married him. For a short time, Carly's life was her dream come true. In the first years of their marriage, she and her husband established habits that they planned to enjoy all their lives; simple things like walking to a local bakery to buy fresh croissants on Friday evenings, then lying in bed Saturday morning reading the paper and drinking coffee and nibbling pastry until noon. In the bliss of living a life of her own design, she forgot about the daily conflict she'd endured before. Then, one by one, and two

Living Your Dream in the Real World

by two, her siblings and their mates followed her example. Inspired by Carly's obvious successes in her chosen city, they purchased homes a few miles away.

While it was intrusive enough to suddenly begin receiving their daily phone calls and drop-in visits, it soon got worse. Carly's parents decided to move, too. So, all the conflict, the family upstaging, and sabotage that Carly had escaped was now in her own back yard. And, since she and her siblings had never given up their roles of obedient children, their parents expected everything to go on as before.

To Carly, their presence required accepting her old role of proving by daily action her gratitude for their "giving up everything" to send her through college. So, despite the demands of her job, a new baby, a husband, and things around her own home to do, Carly felt obliged to go to her parents' house several evenings a week and weekends, either to visit, or to drive them places because they weren't used to freeways. It should come as no surprise that, within a few months, Carly had lost a significant amount of weight and was crying at the *anticipation* of having the phone ring.

One morning, when her son was nearly a year old, Carly awoke with what was becoming a standard headache. But, this time, with it came a thought: I'm sick and tired of being pulled this way and that—I want my own life back! So Carly sought help from a professional therapist, who told her to step aside and re-evaluate her entire family: her parents' role in her life, and her role in theirs. Then she was told to mentally remove herself from the family—to envision what her parents would do if she wasn't around.

What Carly came to realized is that, simply by participating in her parents' expectations, she had become part of the problem. To get back to living her own life, Carly had to quit what she was doing. So, she began by not reacting to her siblings' complaints, or her parents' calls for help. Was it easy? No! Carly says that breaking those lifetime habits was the hardest thing she's ever done. To get her own dream back, it was something she had to do. What's happened since she began backing away from daily, then weekly, obligations? Now, her parents drive themselves. And Carly has had time to look at what she wants to do with the hours she's won back. She's pursuing her dream of becoming a lyricist, so she's taking music lessons, practicing her guitar, taking weekend retreats with her husband and baby, and spending time alone. By moving beyond old habits, beliefs, behaviors, and patterns, Carly's dream is expanding all over again.

Whenever you find yourself slipping back into old habits, beliefs, behaviors, and patterns, journal about the relationships, places, or things that no longer represent the person that you are becoming—or that serve your dream. In which areas do you need to move? Does it call for changing jobs? Re-examining personal or professional relationships?

Attitude Magic

For you maybe all it takes to feel as if your life is fulfilling is a refocusing of what's going on in your life at that moment. While Carly needed to make some changes in her life to feel really fulfilled, sometimes it's just our outlook on life that can be detrimental to us living our dream. Indeed, after Carly examined her atttitude, she found that her perception of, and approach to, her daily living situation was affecting her happiness as much as the situation itself was.

The following affirmations work on adjusting your attitude. Through engaging in a little "attitude magic" you might find that your life only needs some fine-tuning.

* More than anything else, it is my attitude, or mental position, that ensures my ability to realize my dream.

* My attitude toward life determines life's attitude toward me.

* My attitude toward others determines others' attitudes towards me.

* Gandhi said, "You must be the change you wish to see in the world." I must think, act, talk, walk, and conduct myself in all my affairs as the person I wish to become, living in the world I wish to live in.

* The deepest human desire is to be of service to others and to the world. I will adopt an attitude of giving. I will become an energy giver, rather than an energy taker, a constructive rather than a destructive force in all my relationships.

Living Your Dream in the Real World

- ✳ I will consciously work to develop a receptive mind. I will learn from all my experience. As I maintain an attitude of discovery, I know I will unfold like a blossoming flower.

- ✳ I will radiate the attitude of well-being, of confidence, of someone who knows where I am going. I attract what I am.

- ✳ My attitude determines my state of health and well-being. I will focus on health. I will focus on mental clarity and spiritual fulfillment. I will focus on possibilities. I will focus on my dream.

- ✳ If I don't have a dream, my life will be about problems. If I don't relate to others on the level of my dream, my time will be occupied by my problems. By being creative, I will create the life I want.

- ✳ When I nurture a positive attitude, I live in a positive world. For the rest of my life, I will live the dreamer's life. I will practice the magical attitude.

- ✳ I am what I dream. Shifting my attitude is a modern magic wand!

Moving Beyond Excuses

Re-evaluating your life, even looking at your present-day circumstances and finding out what is standing in your way, can bring about mixed emotions. While examining old behavior and habits that can be getting it the way of you being all that you can be is often liberating, frequently the revelations bring us to a standstill. And then we find ourselves making excuses for not addressing them—for not moving on.

A gifted writer stopped writing when she moved out of her parents' home because they were the ones with the computers. Believing that she could not write without a computer, she put her dream of being a novelist on hold. During a session I pointed out that I'd written *three* books without owning a computer. Then I asked, "Have you always made excuses for not reaching a goal, dream, or wish that you've said you want?"

"It's not an excuse! How can I write if I don't have a computer?"

"Many active writers prefer to write in longhand. If you prefer to use a computer, consider renting one," I coached her. End of *that* excuse! You see, she had gotten into the practice of excusing herself. If writing was part of her one dream, she'd find a way! She needs to move through the excuses by making a list of all of the reasons that being a writer frightens her. It could be laziness, fear, or an unwillingness to tell herself the truth. Every dream activator needs to get in touch with the excuses he or she makes. Not taking responsibility for getting beyond them will make progress slower.

Make a list of how many socially acceptable excuses you have made this week, leaving a space between each one. Write about why you used them. In the space between each, describe what truth you could have told yourself, and others.

Correcting Your Course When You Hit a Real-Life Barrier

One of my closest friends is an artist who had had showings of her prints and oils in a number of states. When her first child was born, Alice began finding it difficult to schedule her need to paint with his nap times. Still, it was possible to think, experiment, and finalize a concept before the paint dried. Then came the second child! By the time the third child was born—eleven months after the second—scheduling any time for herself became impossible. Alice's passionate need to create was stronger than ever . . . and her frustration about not filling the emptiness within her was making her crabby.

Realizing that she must find a solution, Alice decided to release her creativity in something that did not involve rapidly drying paint. Since she'd always loved writing, she bought a typewriter. "Rising each morning at 4:30 A.M. to write until 6:30 when my husband and children awake," she recently told her dream coach, "is wonderful. I'd found myself wanting to rush the children through things in the hopes of getting a few moments for myself. Now, I've had my creativity fix and, for the rest of the day, I'm able to relax and *enjoy* being a wife and mother. My life is more because I've allowed time for my dream of being creative." Remember what I said earlier: when you are fulfilled, everyone benefits!

Living Your Dream in the Real World

Regrouping When Things Aren't Going the Way You Planned

And then there's me. Remember the Irish prayer that goes, "May the wind be always at your back"? Well, my dream and I ran into some real challenging headwinds, instead. In addition to the usual family losses, triumphs, and challenges, there came this:

After giving up my teaching career, creating a self-supporting business, and having my first book published, the recession hit California. Earlier, my husband had left teaching and coaching to enter into a partnership specializing in building spec houses. They'd constructed and sold four out of seven very expensive homes just before the floor dropped out from under the building industry. Now, we'd never intended to sell one of the remaining three houses—that one was our dream home, the one in which I'd intended to live the rest of my life.

When notes came due on the last two houses . . . and selling them appeared impossible . . . my husband and I were left to pay for the two partnership mortgages, the final sub-contractors' fees, along with our own mortgage and bills. Desperate to keep the bank from repossessing the two spec houses, we sold our home to partially pay debts incurred by the business. However, it turned out that our house didn't raise enough money. So we withdrew our retirement funds, canceled our private health insurance, then added the small inheritance my husband had received from his mother. Finally, with only our furniture left, everything was paid off. Quite suddenly, there we were at retirement age with no pension, no investments, no home, and the dreams we'd held in our hearts. No doubt about it, this was definitely a tough time! Sometimes tough times are what's needed to find out who you are, what you stand for, and how important your dream really is!

At the age of sixty-three, my husband, no longer the owner of a construction firm, put on a carpenter's apron and headed for the one thing we still owned—a piece of property in another state. Building and selling a house there, we hoped that we would recoup some of our losses. Then came time for my decision: With my company based and established in Southern California, was I to accompany him and relocate my business?

As I saw it, to leave was to put a hold on living my dream. Reality was saying, Pack it in: there's no extra money for an office, staff, or house rental. But I knew better—I just felt it! First of all, I was willing to work eighteen hours a day, if necessary. I was willing to go back to doing things the way I'd done them when I was first married. Moving into a tiny rental, I stayed to continue writing, creating, and managing my consulting firm. Over the years, we'd become financially solvent enough that I'd purchased other people's services. Now, I did everything myself! It was both a wonderful and awful time. And on the most horrible, awful day that terrible year there came a sign that what I had done was right. My second book, *Journaling for Joy,* hit the stands. And then *another* miracle happened in the form of confirmation. Letters began arriving from all over the country from people who'd just purchased my second book to tell me how much my two books had changed their lives. After presentations and talks, people would come to me and thank me for rekindling shattered or delayed dreams, for motivating them to take responsibility for making changes in themselves. From this, I knew that I had been right to stay where I was: concentrating on the work that nurtured my spirit and continued to energize my dream.

Now there were, of course, other options. Both my husband and I could have gone back to teaching. In fact, many people suggested this. He could have taken any number of jobs right here in town. But he chose to go to a neighboring state. My choice was based on knowing that I am on this planet to help others discover their dreams and express myself through the work I love and am trained to do! Had I made excuses, moved at a time when my business needed my total commitment, or taken a job to help get us through, I might not now be writing this book . . . or perhaps the ones to follow. Because I regard remaining true to one's dream of ultimate importance, I want *you* to look upon any challenges coming your way as merely a signal that it is time to review—then renew—your commitment to yourself and your dream. That dream is your destiny. So claim it. Insist upon it!

And, there's always humor in the midst of hardship. While visiting the building site during a holiday, my husband was repairing damage on the third story of a house. Looking down at me from a twenty-foot ladder, he hollered, "Joyce, I want you to know that I'm not *enjoying* my golden years!" True, things

Living Your Dream in the Real World

haven't turned out exactly the way we'd planned, but did we despair? Yes, of course! Have we given up? Never!

Daily Practices When You Get Stuck

Recently in my ongoing journaling group, a woman wrote about feeling stuck and remarked that it was time for her to "put on her power shoes." What she meant was, stepping back into her personal and spirit power.

To get through being stuck, step into your power shoes. Then, take time to:

* Bring yourself back to center through realignment with your dream.

* Embrace living as if your dream is being realized.

* Appreciate the little things that *are* working in your life by recording them in your journal.

* Practice until you perfect the art of noticing the beauty of everyday things: sunlight coming through a window to splash across your desk; washing the car; the march of pansies along a path; the touch of caressing your favorite belongings; the musical tinkling of wind chimes stirred by the breezes.

* Continue to replace any habits that reinforce negativity, any which breed despair. This will lead to taking action that brings you closer to your dream.

When Rita was being pressured to assume the presidency of a local historical society, I asked her what she really wanted to do. Having taken my workshop, she had already partially identified a dream that would eventually affect everyone in the nation, that is, impacting the world through her writing. When she mentioned that she wanted time off from community responsibilities to plan that future, I asked a tongue-in-cheek question. "Well, can you be the president of the United States if you're busy being president of your local historical society?" I said. Rita says as ridiculous a comparison as that was, it made all the difference in the world. "Suddenly everything was very clear," she said. "I could continue doing what I'd always done—which was very important on the local level—or I could recognize that now it's time to move higher." So, she not only removed herself from that organization, Rita left another elected office and a part-time position as a college instructor.

Easy? No. Rita says that "backing out on commitments is humiliating for anyone who prides themselves on being totally dependable." My response? "You might want to take a different view. While all of those positions are extremely valuable, I don't see that you are deserting people. Instead, you are leaving positions that no longer fit with realizing your dream." Did Rita have income to replace that which she gave up? Not within the next two weeks! However, believing that, if she was working toward her own highest good, the highest level authors and experts would come to her. Have they? Yes! Currently, she is ghosting a book for two psychiatrists, editing one for an attorney and another for a home nursing specialist. Will these books assist and empower others to change the world? Absolutely! In addition, Rita is experiencing the thrill of doing precisely what she knows she was put on this planet to do!

Daily questions to ask and take to your journal.
- ★ *What am I doing that is blocking my progress?*
- ★ *What am I thinking that is blocking my forward movement?*
- ★ *What am I willing to give up to follow my dream?*
- ★ *What is it that I must overcome?*
- ★ *What is my plan?*

As an addendum, whenever I am blocked I repeat the following words as many times as needed to get me where I want to be:

> I embrace and release all those past events, experiences, and beliefs that keep me from my dream. I send them toward the light with love, and thank them for what they have taught me.

Living Your Dream in the Real World

By embracing, releasing, and acknowledging I am free from any unwanted influences.

Moving Beyond Giving Up

Each of us has had moments of glory. Despite that, however, we have at one time or another, come to the point of giving up. Don't do that! Where there's a dream, there's a way, and, without a dream, no one is fully alive. Sitting here, writing and rewriting this book, it momentarily seems too demanding. But, remembering the celebrations thrown for me upon the publication of earlier books—and all the letters of gratitude that I've received—inspire me to go on beyond the frustration of *these* burdensome days and weeks. So, during times of boredom, or fatigue, or hopelessness, I force myself to recall earlier "moments of glory." I then write them all down. When you find yourself wanting to give up, recall your moment of glory. Then:

On your art pad or in your journal, list in chronological order your glorious moments and those who believed in you at the time: parents, coaches, mentors, teachers, friends, relatives, or authority figures.

My friend Phyllis knew from the time she was a child, retreating under the kitchen table with pencils and paper at six years of age, that she was going to be a writer. Between that childhood and now, at sixty-seven, she has raised a family and worked in many jobs that always provided her with the opportunity to utilize her writing skills. Now a professional fund-raiser, she is putting the finishing touches on a novel.

Phyllis is one of those few fortunate souls who knew what she wanted to do at a young age. And it also took her a whole lifetime to get back to her original dream. While it's absolutely fine to live life and accomplish a whole host of other fulfilling tasks before you answer to your dream, it's funny how the heart's desire always surfaces and makes itself known.

Chances are you had an inkling of what you wanted to do with your life early on. Maybe you ignored your dreams for awhile. Maybe now you are coming into your dream late in life (and "late" is a relative term!), or, more than likely, you're feeling stuck because you haven't yet listened to your innermost calling.

If you find yourself in a place where you feel like giving up, spend some time carefully examining the root of your dream. You're sure to find that the seeds for those dreams were planted earlier in life, and perhaps some of your frustrations are simply the lack of attention to those dreams and their inability to surface.

1. *Identify at what age you first knew the dream that you are working on now. (Phyllis was six.)*

2. *When were you first acknowledged for being able to do that? (Phyllis was in first grade when a teacher praised her stories.)*

3. *What natural skills are you using? (Phyllis was a born writer, but she's never stopped honing her skills.)*

4. *How are you now aligning with your dream? (Phyllis worked only in jobs directly involved in, or paralleling, her dream.)*

5. *Are your feelings of being stuck or frustrated directly related to you not fulfilling your most coveted dreams?*

Moving Past the Advice and Opinions of Others

You've made up your mind. You are in the process of fine-tuning your plans, and taking your latest step toward your dream. And then, for no apparent reason, you are stopped in your tracks by recalling the well-meant counsel or warnings of others. That is what happened to one of my clients—the owner of a charming specialty bookstore.

Previously, school district librarian Karl had a twenty-year history of depression and severe headaches. Since opening a specialty bookstore two years ago, he has been free of all illness. But, while the shop supports his staff, the business will take a year or two more before it provides enough money to pay him an impressive salary. His retired teacher wife has complained since the bookstore opened that he was indulging in a whim . . . that he has had no background or training for developing a successful business. To exhibit her lack

Living Your Dream in the Real World

of faith in him, Helen has insisted upon coming out of retirement and going back to teaching. However, the position she accepted was in another town some hundred miles away. To her, it made sense for them to move because hers was the job that was providing a steady income.

Unwilling to do this, Karl was nevertheless sensitive to his wife's needs. However, his bookstore wasn't losing money . . . and if Helen hadn't gone back to teaching, they would have had enough money in retirement funds to allow a certain amount of risk. But for Helen, who lives in what she considers to be "the real world," it is illogical to take these kinds of chances. Practical Helen is even willing to drive the two hundred miles each day. Karl's brother sides with Helen. "You should be grateful to have a wife who is willing to safeguard your security," he told Karl. So, in addition to being a financial failure, it seems that Karl is ungrateful and selfish.

Will more explanation help Helen understand Karl's need to test himself—to grow? Just as important, without the challenge of making the bookstore a success, will Karl return to bouts of depression and debilitating headaches? He wonders. He also worries: Maybe Helen is right and he is a terrible businessman. Maybe his brother is right: Is he foolish to endanger a marriage of thirty-five years? My recommendation is that Karl listen to *himself*—it is imperative that he determine what he *needs* as well as to know what he *wants*. Then, he is to acknowledge Helen for providing the stability that she needs to do for *herself*! He, after all, did not ask her to go back to work—he didn't even think it was necessary. Her peace of mind is important to him, so he has thanked her for what she is doing; and continually acknowledges her for taking care of herself. At this point, Karl is not only doing that, he has also hired a business consultant to meet with him monthly for counseling and advice. Karl is, you see, every bit as practical as Helen. By listening to her and his brother, he realized that he might do more to guarantee success in his dream.

Rarely do any of us progress without giving up something, and that is what Helen is doing although she most likely doesn't know it. Helen's fear comes because Karl's idea of retirement turned out to be different from hers. After a year of staying around the house, he decided to do what he'd always wanted to do—open a small specialty bookstore. Threatened by this, Helen sincerely feels that she has to be the responsible one. Who else is going to take care of them should his pie in the sky dream not work?

For Helen, it is a matter of winning. If Karl continues to operate his bookstore, she is going to have to acknowledge that he is more capable, brighter, and has more business sense than she wanted to admit. She will observe this by watching how willing he is to make his dream come true.

Remember when I said that we must always work toward the betterment of all involved? If Karl gives in and gets rid of the bookstore, it is very likely that he will return to states of depression and debilitating headaches. To date, his decision is made. As Karl's dream coach, I'm confident that he will succeed. Helen raises other questions. How soon will it be before she begins to resent spending four hours each day driving back and forth to work? Will she be able to see that she can join Karl in his dream by aligning with it? As a teacher, she is an expert in organization, creating exciting learning environments . . . even in gift wrapping purchased books. She created her part of the dilemma by jumping to the conclusion that Karl was jeopardizing their retirement funds. She's written her own lesson. Learning what she needs to know is her choice.

Learning to Prescribe for Yourself

Whenever you perceive something in your life to be a problem, shift your thinking and look upon the situation as an opportunity, as a lesson, as an exercise in learning. Once you understand what you are learning, move on. In the future, you must always first identify the lesson, determine what is to be learned, then prescribe how you're to use the lesson and continue your journey. The important thing to remember when it is your lesson is that you are the only one who has the final answers. No one else in this world knows better than you what's in your heart and what will lead you to your dream.

In a moment of desperate whimsy back when my life seemed full of "lessons" I actually had note pads printed with a pharmaceutical RX on them. Silly as it seems, it forced me to look at things with a more critical eye. By writing my lessons, then my options, on a prescription pad, I began prescribing workable solutions. Meditating on those prescriptions during long walks alone and through writing in my journal, I'd release everything to my spirit power for final solution. I suggested this practice to all my clients.

Notifying Yourself and Others if Your Focus Changes

In the 1920s, when seven-year-old Bud Lueck visited his first museum, the curator placed a rock in his hand and said, "This is over a million years old." Lueck remembers, "That's when I fell in love with old!" Collecting relics and artifacts quickly became Lueck's obsession, as did becoming a curator. But, in school smack dab in the middle of the Great Depression, he was advised to go into something more practical instead. "Use your abilities in math and science to make a great deal of money," the counselor recommended. "Keep adding to your collections, then, build your own museum!" Eventually, that is exactly what Bud Lueck did. But, first, he collected and contributed to other museums.

By building a number of successful sheet metal businesses, he was making the kind of money it took to purchase the beautiful items he wanted to collect. Specializing in artifacts from North and South America, Lueck and his wife traveled the length and breadth of the continent over the years, purchasing and collecting artifacts illustrating prehistoric artisans' skill in everything from chipping flint to pottery and basket-making, from decorative feather to beadwork. One large collection he was able to purchase once belonged to Seattle's well-known collector, Daddy Stanley. And all the time, Lueck's businesses continued growing, aided by the invention of a copper drain, designed especially for flat industrial roofs. Then, over forty years after he'd begun collecting and donating items to other museums, his vision changed.

Re-evaluating where he was—and where he was going—Lueck decided to stop donating to other museums and build his own. And, in 1993, his revised dream came true: Grossmont/Cuyamaca College District, seventeen miles inland from San Diego, donated a prime piece of land for his use. With additional financial help from his adult children, friends, and community supporters, the spectacular Heritage of the America's Museum opened on January 20, 1993.

Not only were four wings necessary to house his collection, the building itself was designed by Lueck. Inside, all of the display cabinets are also his handiwork. Outside, surrounded by palms—grown from seedlings by the Luecks—the museum is today host to busloads of children . . . some of whom for the first time get to hold a million-year-old rock in their small hands.

Is the museum worth all the time, money, and planning? Is it worth the years of propositions made and denied? Worth the setbacks and disappointments?

"Absolutely," says Lueck. "There were times when I ran into obstacles and they set me back a day or two—maybe a month. But I never lost sight of where I was going." So, trusting that—some day—his museum would be a reality, Lueck convinced others to believe in his dream by continuing to collect, plan, travel, and study. Persistence over five decades paid off; not just in the long run, but all along the way. Bud's enthusiasm captured the interest of his wife, his children, and grandchildren, too. As for the community—they now have a treasure right in their own neighborhood; both in the collections and in Bud and Bernadette, too, because they are in the museum six days a week, leading tours.

So, share any change in attitude or direction with those on your empowerment team, your friends, and the community at large. By notifying them, you receive the encouragement that you might need to keep going. Just as you can't build museums without the help of others, you can't be president of the United States if you are too busy doing what you've done before!

To keep a close check on yourself, step back and observe where you are right now. Write down answers in your journal to the following:

* *How many times have I altered my dream, or my focus, since I began reading this book?*

* *Have I notified anyone of these changes?*

* *Do I want/need to notify them now?*

* *Whom do I want to notify?*

* *By what method?*

* *How do I want them to react?*

* *What will I want them to do?*

Living Your Dream in the Real World

Visualizing Yourself Back Into Good Times

Many programs recommend using creative visualization these days, and for good reason! Athletes are encouraged to "picture" themselves achieving more than they have previously thought possible. Motivational speakers often suggest to their audiences that the first step toward achievement lies in envisioning themselves doing what they've always wanted. The results of visualization are often rewarding and, sometimes, almost miraculous. Time and again, people have amazed themselves by actually accomplishing what they've previously only hoped for. If you haven't tried picturing yourself realizing and celebrating your dream, don't worry that—logically—envisioning yourself to success doesn't make sense. Just know that your mind and body working together can make your dream a reality. So, if you haven't been doing so all along, it's time to trust your own intentions.

You can't see what you can't see—to give physical representation to what is in your mind's eye, pull out your art pad—you're going to assemble a Destination Board to determine where you are going. Over the next month or two, snip words and pictures from magazines and brochures to reflect what you want to achieve and possess. Collecting things that represent what you want to experience for mind, body, and spirit, glue them onto your Destination Board. Look at this, the physical realities in the real world—and they are all yours for the asking . . . and the working.

Going Beyond Your Own Perceptions

For anyone having difficulty working with things they can't see, measure, or weigh, I can only say that there are many things that I've never witnessed that I believe. For instance, I've never encountered an angel, yet I believe the millions who say that they have. I'm not able to wire a house, and I fully expect the dishwasher to work when I turn the knob. So look at your mental energy as something at the other end of your mental power switch. Envision it! By accepting the something out there beyond your own perception and line of sight, *you can expect* your energy to move the instant you turn it on. Use that energy to fire up your creativity, to further illuminate your path, to incorporate your wishes into your ever-changing life.

After years of doing this, I can actually *feel* energy circulating within me. As the current courses through me, it carries me to the place where my ideas originate. And because I embrace that flow, there is a massive change in my energy level. If I can do it, so can every dream activator alive! The key is to know your highest dream, then make the commitment to use all of your own powers to bring it about. Tell others what you intend to do, then begin doing the work! That is when the magic begins.

Once this begins, you discover that, although there will always be some sort of obstacle—a loan to secure, a computer to purchase, a language to master—earlier limits are gone. When asked how she transcends the limits of the human body while dancing, ballerina Nadia Sonenburg replied, "I let the music play *me!*" Just as sculptors say the statue already existed in the stone, artists frequently admit, "I didn't paint this picture, it was inside of me just waiting to get out." In the same way, many authors and songwriters pay homage to an indefinable something deep within them that is the source of their works. In much the same way, in-touch architects and carpenters use spatial vision to interpret what their clients want, and mechanics sense what's wrong with engines. All transcend their training and conspicuous knowledge to tap into another dimension. From there, they can foresee the highest need and the highest good. So, what are hunches, reality, creativity but other words for miracles, and magic! When energized, each becomes an aspect of your conscious commitment to yourself. So, activate the magic in you by placing yourself in your highest dream. Believe in what you created. Then get on with getting it!

To do that, take a few minutes to join me as I return to a time of childhood belief in magic and miracles. Sit with me for a moment in the silence as I retreat inward. Then, lifting a mental wand, swoosh it around in front of you. You may discover, as I have, that suddenly you are free from having to think sequentially. In that instant it becomes all right to embrace everything that—on the face of it—appears illogical. No longer must your creative wondering be slowed by tried-and-true, step-by-step processes established by someone else. That is because, by returning to a state of childlike wondering, you can accept what the world regards as sleight-of-hand. So, believe alchemy is possible: that an ugly toad of a person can be transformed into a handsome, loving human being; that you can manifest anything that you want. Believing in that kind of thinking that transforms you—that frees your creative spirit— generating the purity of energy you need/want to obtain a powerful shift beyond your usual view of things.

Now, recording in your journal or drawing on your art pad, answer these questions:

★ What did I feel?

★ What else did I experience?

★ Have I gained sudden clarity on any aspect of my dream?

★ How will this change the way I have viewed things?

★ How is this going to alter what I am doing?

★ What results can I see coming from all this?

This exercise is excellent when you feel down when you'd rather be up. When living in the real world seems tough.

Living Congruently with the Dream

In bad times and good, each of us needs to remind ourselves to live every day as if our dream was already realized. The world is full of people who say they want to be one thing, but act another. If you want to be an executive, accept total responsibility and administer accordingly. If you want to be a priest or healer, practice behaving with the purest of intent and action every day of your life. If you want to be a politician, exemplify what public servants ought to be by living an honest, responsible life. Whatever it is you want to become, ask yourself throughout the day, "Am I at this very moment living compatibly with my dream and dream self?"

Combining personal power and spirit energy must be practiced from moment to moment. That means walking in your strength, and wearing it for everyone to see. To illustrate, one of my favorite beliefs is, "Wear the right costume, and the part plays itself." In other words, if you are to fully accept the power of what you want to become, you'll need to practice wearing the right outfit. The force of this should never be underestimated, as the following examples show.

Recently, I organized a visit to an expensive apparel shop in La Jolla, California, for a dozen men and women interested in empowering themselves so they might achieve their dreams. I'd arranged for store personnel to receive us after hours. Also there were make-up artists, hair stylists, and professional dressers experienced in providing professional people with the proper clothing. When "finished," each member of the group modeled his or her new self for the rest of us. What an experience!

Appearances make *such* a difference: in each instance, the person emerging from the dressing room was not the same as the one who had gone in. A school secretary emerged as the polished professional she said she wanted to become. But it wasn't just the hair-do, or the beautiful suit—she walked differently, held her head at a different angle. In that suit, she was what she wanted to be.

A female attorney, tired of suppressing her femininity, had exchanged her ultra-conservative, severely tailored suit for a softer, but still professionally appropriate, jacket-dress ensemble. Her previously untouched face was lightly enhanced with subdued eye-shadow, blush, and lipstick. Revealed were surprisingly blue eyes and astonishing cheekbones. Would attractiveness hamper her in the courtroom? Male attorneys in the group were firm in their belief that it would not!

Out from the dressing room came a man who was there only because his wife insisted. While all of us knew that he was employed by his wife's family, and that he hated the job, none of us knew how he dressed for the job. We had only seen him in what we assumed was after-work clothing: jeans, sneakers, and a sweatshirt. But the dresser, knowing his dream of becoming a college instructor, had dressed him in a tweed sports coat, khaki slacks, and loafers. It caught everyone by surprise. Just as quickly, they accepted what they saw. And their reaction solidified his determination to get an advanced degree and teach history. In a matter of minutes, he moved beyond obstacles to work on his dream. And some of those who saw the transformation became members of his empowerment team.

Living Your Dream in the Real World

Did permanent change come to everyone that night? Interestingly, all of the men so loved wearing their new costumes that they purchased them and moved forward. It was the women who held back, unwilling—or unable—to accept responsibility for making their dreams come true. Some of them worried about what their husbands would say to any changes they might make. Others worried that their husbands would be upset by the cost of the clothing. In fact, two of them had become so anxious about even considering such changes, that they became physically ill while trying on the clothing. But in the weeks that followed, four women processed the supportive reactions they'd received that night and went back to purchase their "costumes." What this illustrates is that the mere act of "trying on" what you'd like to become is a step in the right direction. By doing this repeatedly, you begin making your dream come true. Activate your personal and spirit power by wearing the appropriate attire. Make it a habit!

Another way of redefining an outward manifestation of your changing spirit is by updating your home and office. First of all, get rid of everything that doesn't fit who and where you want to be. If you want an elegant life, better to serve salt from its original container than to continue using plastic shakers. But maybe all you need is to change things around. A friend of mine found a whole new way of using what she already had by reading a book on Feng Shui, the ancient Japanese art of activating personal and corporate power through furniture arrangement. Simply turning her desk so that she *faced* the door, instead of having her back to it, transformed the energy of her office. Moving color around and using mirrors added to the circulation of that energy. Sound trendy? Some of America's most successful corporations hire Feng Shui experts to arrange their furnishings! If they're investing in activating "alternate" energies, why can't you? If, however, you can't afford to make any big changes, cut out photos of the house, furnishings, or office you plan to have one day. Frame them and hang them on the wall. Collect other pictures that further clarify what you want and hang them, too.

The same goes for your automobile. Sell it and buy another, paint your present car, visit a car parts store to purchase emblems of the car you plan to buy when your dream is realized—glue them in their proper place on the old buggy, restore the chrome, buy a new license plate holder, change your route to and from work, and/or begin shopping at different stores. Each small outer conversion reflects the inner changes you are making to live compatibly with your dream.

It is impossible to manifest your dream unless you've moved beyond all that has held you back. By activating personal and spirit power, by using your creative energy, by working for the highest good of all involved, by dedicating yourself to becoming the very best that you can be, you find yourself aligned with the highest in a life that suddenly becomes simpler. That's because, with your dream blessing everything you are doing, you are no longer afraid of anything or anyone. So, whether you have fully identified your dream, recognize only part of it, or are moving forward in response to an inner feeling about it, let's celebrate what you've accomplished in the *real* world of dreams.

Never Again . . .

No longer afraid of reaching for your dream, never again will you allow the "real" world to lower the curtain on it, or you. By always aligning with the highest in life, you place yourself among life's celebrants. When journaling about what it means to live your life and your dream consistently and simultaneously, consider the concept that these two realities really *merge*. It's not as if you have to life your life and your dream separately; quite the contrary, the two are uniquely intertwined to create your own special place in the world.

With everything you've learned about yourself and the real world, you are ready to move beyond anything that does not directly affect the realization of your dream. Describe the components of your life that you are no longer willing to allow affect your dream.

Starting on page 21 of chapter 1, you wrote your story of the things you wanted in your life. Now, go back and cross off everything that is no longer congruent. Add whatever you forgot to include.

Living Your Dream in the Real World

Make the Dream Real... Make it Yours

Living your dream in the real world now becomes natural. Each and every experience becomes significant as you travel within your own adventure.

How do you notice that there is really no clear distinction between the "real" world and your dream, and in what ways does it feel wonderful and second-nature to fill your day with your dreamwork?

Living Your Dream in the Real World

Rejoice. You've made many new and bountiful changes in yourself. By living congruently with your claimed reality you are continuously activating your dreams.

CHAPTER 6

Celebrating Your Dream

WHEN WAS THE LAST TIME YOU CELEBRATED—REALLY CELEBRATED someone's birthday, a friend getting a new job, or a big change in your own life? At which of those celebrations did you achieve the highest state of merrymaking? Is it possible that there is an even higher state?

> Celebrating each forward movement—no matter how small or seemingly insignificant—opens the door to becoming increasingly in touch with spiritual and physical fulfillment. Eventually, you find yourself living each day of your life in a state of celebration.

"But," you say, "wanting to live *constantly* in celebration is not only unrealistic, it's frivolous—even superficial. Anyway, who has the time? And, wouldn't celebrating all the time sap your energy for enjoying completion of the big stuff?" Well, it depends upon what you consider to be acts and states of celebration. From Eastern philosophies we have learned that it is desirable to live in the now—to be present, right now, wherever we are. People have removed themselves so much from being present in the moment that all they can do is project, plan, collect, and deal with "musts" around them. This is most obvious in those retirees who can't accept that "some day" has finally arrived and find it terrifying to actually spend the money they've saved. Those who are younger often need to just as consciously get beyond time and money limitations by rediscovering, then redefining, themselves *even without* the security of tomorrow. Does that mean that you should cancel your insurance and stop investing for the years ahead? Emphatically not! I'm just saying that it is essential for your inner growth and power to not get so caught up in preparing for tomorrow that you lose today.

How Have You Celebrated Up to Now?

When you were young, the mere act of splashing paint on paper was one sort of celebration. Having it hung on the refrigerator was another. Many adults find a release of great joy in creating, although their art may not be gallery quality and their poetry may be seen only by themselves. What such creativity provides is pleasure and accomplishment. *Notice and remember* moments like these in your life.

Think back to the last time your threw a really terrific party, shared a precious moment, purchased a gift for someone who did not expect it, rejoiced in someone else's success. Each of those were a celebration!

Make a list of those occasions that filled you with joy or satisfaction. Describe for yourself how each was celebrated, and the feelings you experienced. Determine what brought you into those elevated states of excitement? How long did it last? Did it last for a minute or two? An hour? Weeks? Months? Years? In thinking and writing about those occasions, noting how you felt afterward, and the duration of those feelings, you capture what you've learned from those experiences. To get you started, consider these:

- ★ *Birthdays*
- ★ *Holidays*
- ★ *First touchdowns/home runs/baskets*
- ★ *Passing a test*
- ★ *Starting of menses*
- ★ *Getting a driver's license*
- ★ *Graduations*

- *First sexual experiences*
- *Marriage*
- *Birth of a child*
- *Promotions*
- *An original idea or creation*
- *Recognition for having made a contribution*
- *Unacknowledged contributions*
- *Member of a winning team*
- *Religious ceremonies*
- *Life transitions*
- *A problem solved*
- *Recovery from illness or addiction*

When asked about ways in which such occasions, events, passages have been celebrated, people come up with some really simple means of acknowledgment: telling jokes, singing in the shower, playing music extra loud, buying an ice cream cone, or writing a poem like my client Lissa did:

I SING A SONG OF CELEBRATION

I sing of sunsets, silly hats
Somber moments, midnight chats
Walks on beaches and in parks
Oohs and aahs for wolves and sharks
Flickering candles, wedding bells
Laughter, love, and magic spells.

Others write about celebration in different ways:

Celebrating means a gleeful party with lots of balloons. It's the sparkle, the pageantry, the Christmas, the birthdays.

Celebrating Your Dream

Celebration is a reward—you know, a ribbon—or a trip.

Enjoying the moment with no worry about the past or future, and sharing that joy with others.

Celebration to me includes events, joyful experiences marking a specific issue, life milestone, or giving meaning and significance to the beginning and ending of one of life's transitions. But in the bigger sense, celebration is more than an event: it is an attitude; a joyful approach to all of life. Being able to embrace and experience authentically the whole range of feelings. Being fully alive. Accepting with enthusiasm where I am moment to moment. Celebration is my commitment to life and living.

Do you recall Myra the woman whose house, and life, were in total disorder? Well, five years later, Myra has not only achieved all of the goals she first established, she has become a happier, more fulfilled person. In her words you can see the change available to anyone willing to work toward being the most of who they can be. Myra is a shining example of what happens when you identify a dream, work unceasingly toward its accomplishment, and learn how to celebrate each step along the way.

The word *celebration* brings to mind past parties and reunions, lively activities involving family and friends, all which required lots of preparation and considerable work. But celebration today means something very different to me. More and more, I'm finding a way of rejoicing that does not include lots of people. It is a new sense of freedom; an aloneness accompanied by excitement, fear, and change. It is a solo celebration—an adventure into me and who I am. In other words, I celebrate what is important to

me in a powerful, quieter way. Now I appreciate
simpler pleasures, like those reflected in a smile or
kind word, a gentleness and caring heart, a shared
intimacy with my children.

*Now, look back at what you've discovered so far about your own
experiences. What did your celebrations have in common? How were they
different? What are your talents as a celebrator? What celebrating skills have
you developed? What objects and activities help to trigger your celebration
memories and recreate the spirit? Write a summary of what you have learned
about the ways in which you celebrate.*

*Write about where you are now, versus where you want to be in four
months, in six months, in a year, in five years. Share those ideas with your
empowerment team and dream coach. Discuss all implications. Then, having done
all this, write a short paragraph summarizing your thoughts on an index card.
Post the card on the dashboard of your car, or on a mirror, or other prominent
place where you will notice it often. As the days go by, observe your reactions to
seeing it: Are your ideas on celebration expanding from day to day? As they do,
you will need to reflect this by altering, or adding to, your card. In fact, you will
probably want to write a new card. Or cards!*

Soaring in the New Dimension: The Fireworks Begin!

Having examined your own feelings toward personal achievement and
celebration, do you better understand the reward/gratification processes you
have already established for yourself? It is through understanding them that you
further actuate your dreams. As a dream activator, you operate in a new
dimension—by following your mission, you rocket into the realm of the
extraordinary. Even there, however, negative influences from outside can affect
you if you allow them to. To protect yourself from doubt and opposition,
program your inner spirit each night to awaken you each morning caught up in
the wonder and hope of your dreams. Throughout the day, if needed, call upon
that energetic exuberance to renew you.

Celebrating Your Dream

Having done so much to define and claim your dream, you've embraced more power than you suspected was available. Encouraged to identify your own personal kinds of celebration, you now find that it's time to integrate what you've learned.

Take time right now to dust off your mental ribbons, balloons, and sparklers while you are getting out both a gold and a silver pen; today is the day your words take on a special shine, so describe what you are feeling.

It is said that the only mind you can ever change is your own. However, you know better than most that as you alter *your* thinking and doing, everything and everyone around you changes, too! Unity minister and author Emmet Fox talks about this in describing the method of building a "mental equivalent" as the means by which a person, community, or nation achieves innermost desires. Once again, for dream activators to get what is wanted, they must create a mental image of themselves living their dream.

To give you another exercise in creating that imaging, answer the next set of questions to forever change your life. As you take the next week to think, write about, review, change, and discuss the first sixteen questions with your empowerment team or dream coach, you are becoming more specific in building the mental equivalent of what it is you want to celebrate.

1. *What is the highest dream you want to celebrate in this lifetime?*

2. *What is your passion?*

3. *What is it that you know you were born to do?*

4. *How do you know that you were born to celebrate your dream?*

5. *In what ways does your dream involve celebration?*

6. *How will celebrating your dream impact you and the universe?*

7. *What do you need to do to realize and celebrate your dream?*

8. *What do you want to do to realize and celebrate your dream?*

9. *What do you choose to do to realize and celebrate your dream?*

10. *What are your opportunities/challenges for growth?*

11. Why is realizing and celebrating this dream so important to you?

12. Did you use any excuses today? What were they? In what ways did they serve you?

13. In which ways, today, have you acted in accordance with what you say you want?

14. Who taught you to claim your highest dream? Who taught you to accept your personal power? Your spirit energy? What do your answers suggest to you now?

15. Are you, right now, modeling the behavior of a person accepting his or her power and celebrating his or her highest dream? If yes, how? If no, why not?

16. How did you accept your power today and celebrate your highest dream?

Over the next week or two, consider the following:

17. If you had just arrived on this planet and your job was to teach others to celebrate their highest dream, what would you teach them? And how would you plan to teach them?

Having answered the first seventeen questions, devote at least a week to thinking about, writing, and discussing the last four:

18. As a practicing celebrant, what evidence do you want each day that you are claiming and celebrating your dream?

19. Think ahead to when you attain your dream and write those questions you will be asked by television and radio interviewers on celebration. Then go back and answer each question.

20. Catch yourself being joyful. Every day for at least a month (or for the rest of your life), write what you felt like celebrating, what you thought about celebrating, what you did and with whom, and how you felt about the celebration process.

21. List one hundred smaller dreams that will empower you to realize your ultimate dream. When you finish, reread your list and star those you are truly committed to doing.

Celebrating Your Dream

When you are through with all twenty-one questions, highlight what you want to consider in more depth. Copy questions or directives that you want to think and write about onto a clean sheet of paper for further review. Draw fireworks next to those you want to activate or enact right now. Each day, write one of them onto a card and take it with you so that you can think about it off and on during the day.

To make these active reminders a part of your everyday life, carry them on your person (proximity to skin generates a kind of mental osmosis). So carry them in a pocket . . . tuck them in a bra . . . pin them on underwear. For home wear, print them on a T-shirt. But *print them upside down* so *you* can read them. Leave room so that you can update as you and your dream evolve. Celebrate that list. Then, because you will soon have many opportunities to ignite the next stage of celebration, review your activators often. Write new answers to the foregoing questions to reflect each new turn of your thinking. With each one, you grow more free—more powerful.

However, along with your increasing freedom come reminders of what may have been new boundaries just weeks ago—the importance of always being honest and above-board about your intent, and achieving your goals only through shared personal and spirit power. Only then—when the perimeters of appropriate behavior are honored—does your own freedom grow. Because real empowerment comes with the inner peace that tells you that you are pursuing your dream in harmony with the universe, you know that you can fulfill yourself. Continue living the following rules to establish boundaries that will establish a permanent state of independence and increasing incidents of joy.

1] Live from your *highest dream* every moment of every day.

2] Live from the excitement of knowing every life experience is a learning experience.

3] Live from the perspective of discovery.

4] Live by embracing the change that comes with clarity.

5] Live from telling your highest truth.

6] Live from your highest universal self each moment of every day.

7] Live for, from, and in your passion.

8] Live from knowing what you were born to do.

9] Live from the values, habits, beliefs, and actuators that are in alignment with the realization of your dream.

10] Live in the purest expression of your personal power and spirit energy.

11] Live from knowing everything in your life is an opportunity to use those powers.

12] Live to celebrate liberating and using your powers well!

Establishing and Staying in the NOW

I love that my clients say to me, "I am so glad that when we are together you focus completely upon *me*." By that, they mean that I remember what they've said in the past, and connect that information with what they are saying in the now. That is because I do not allow family concerns, professional challenges, or other clients' problems to intrude upon the time I am spending with the client-of-the-moment. Neither do I allow my professional life to color my enjoyment of my family. In other words, I don't pack outside interests into what is happening right now. However, I believe that before any of us can do that, we must learn to live in the *how*. By that I mean, start noticing how you behave when something happens that makes you happy. Because our reactions are usually spontaneous, we don't give them their due. Catch yourself smiling, singing, whistling, or humming and recognize that these actions are reflections of inner joy. Then go back to what prompted the smiles and whistles to discover what it is that you are celebrating—rain after a dry spell, a child's pleasure, a neatly mown yard, freshly polished silver, recently capped teeth, or the smell of fresh coffee.

Starting right now, keep a list of small, commonplace events or situations that produce mini-celebrations because they bring hundreds of satisfactory seconds of everyday joy in life.

Celebrating Your Dream

Recently, I was on my way into our community library. On either side of the walk are rows of well-tended rose bushes. Always, their bright blooms give me a sense of well-being. As I walked up the steps, one particular flower caught my attention. Maybe it was the delicacy of its pinkness, maybe the darker hue rimming the outer edge of its petals that captivated me. At any rate, I stopped, leaned down to smell it, then studied its every furl and curl. "Thank you," I whispered, "for enriching my life." Then, aware of the way my spirit had embraced that flower's beauty, I continued on into the library with an inner sense of being in the right place at the right time—part of my dream because when I'm in my right place, I affect those around me.

Benefiting Others

What wonderful, perfectly normal thing grabbed your attention yesterday? Your children cheerfully squabbling over morning cereal? Be glad that they are alive and healthy! And know that their freedom to agree or disagree reflects your acceptance of them as normal children—when you are in your right place, they are too! Celebrate that! And in the same way, celebrate your orderly in and out baskets: how wonderful to see the day's chores so clearly delineated so that you have time to concentrate upon your dream. A perfectly ironed shirt: how good it smells and looks. So, celebrate having chores that allow your mind to run free, that benefit those close to you, and provide time to contemplate a dream! And celebrate making, or having, dinner: the satisfaction that comes with spending part of the evening over a pleasant meal!

One of the more pleasant benefits of my having written *Live Your Dream* has been in receiving a newly published book by another author. Inside, on the title page, she had written a beautiful thank you because it was through reading my book and doing the exercises that she had realized her dream of authoring her book. Who wouldn't celebrate that? And, who wouldn't celebrate hearing from a young woman who'd gone from writing poetry for herself to writing for a local newspaper, to leaving a message on my machine that she'd just won the San Diego Press Club Award for the best non-daily article of the year? And, just recently, I attended the opening of a private art gallery where I was publicly acknowledged by the owner as providing the structure for realizing his dream. Celebrate? I celebrate all the time!

Take time right this minute to list what it is around you that brings you pleasure. Add to each instance the feelings you experience when thinking about them.

Simply by consciously recognizing that which is wonderful to you, you elevate yourself into a state of celebration.

Now, make a list of experiences and feelings you might never have considered celebrating before. One that you may want to include is feeling alone. Just think about celebrating being all by yourself! Then think of the relaxation that comes with monotony. Isn't it lulling to do nothing? And doesn't having nothing to do or think or be sometimes refuel you so that you can get back to something meaningful? Try investigating the words "sad," "excited," and "fearful." When your list is completed, review how far you have come from your initial reaction to seeing those experiences and feelings written in words. Next, note how each of those feelings and attitudes forward your dream.

Celebrating the Passion of Life

Remember a time when you went through the *process* of celebrating but felt something was missing. Maybe you'd attended an event or party where people were supposed to be rejoicing but you detected no real spirit of camaraderie or joy. And you noticed that because everyone was only pretending, they drank a little too much and laughed a bit too hard to make up for the loss. In that company, instead of experiencing real thrill and jubilation, you ended up being uncomfortable because you knew that you were participating in a charade.

In your journal, list what wasn't there, or was wrong. If you could go back and change anything, what would it be?

Now, remember events that you have wholeheartedly celebrated. For instance, how do you act when your favorite candidate or team wins? How do you feel? What do you experience when watching the perfection of a dancer's leap, the perfect stroke of an artist's brush, the first frost of the year, the changing colors of migratory birds, a baby's first smile? Is your exhilaration at witnessing these occurrences not a form of celebration?

Not all celebrations are felt with the same intensity or duration; appreciating the fleeting beauty of a rose, for instance, may not compare with the life-long thrill of having won a Pulitzer. We can increase our awareness of prizing the everyday ordinaryness of human achievement—for each carries us forward in awareness, and with awareness we draw closer to our dream. How many times have you experienced the excitement that comes in doing something well, the elation that accompanies a memorable sunrise, or the enchantment of an unfolding new love? How many times after those experiences were you uplifted simply by remembering? By acknowledging and retaining the joys of the past, we produce *and celebrate* them again and again. Prior thrills encourage us to anticipate future joys of our own making. So let's move ahead by projecting those "high" feelings you will experience upon the achievement of your dream. Imagine yourself at the head of a grand parade; envision being honored by your favorite charity, or branch of government. How do you feel?

"Wait a minute!" you say. "To attain and maintain such a high-energy state implies a revolution in the customary way the world works." How true! Without problems to focus on, what would the world's citizenry think about? What would there be for any of us to do? Would we just sit around all day, daydreaming or watching TV? Without wars and starvation and the homeless, would life become empty and meaningless? Or, is it possible that those things continue to exist because, *subconsciously,* most of us fear that without them we would be left with nothing to do? *Not to those of us working on our dreams.* Not to those of us taking time to celebrate the process! You might be interested in what some dream activators have discovered as they worked toward realizing their dreams. People from many walks of life have shared their notions of celebration with me. Here are some of their replies:

> Celebration means joyful living, breathing out with as much love and joy, and taking in with as much excitement and energy, as every cell of your body can hold.

To me, celebration is being open and willing to listen and learn, to move and keep moving, to have complete trust as I travel along the path toward a new beginning. To have, like the child's church song, "The joy, joy, joy, joy down in my heart; down in my heart to stay." Celebration is appreciation.

Openness! Life! Music! Laughter! Connection!

Celebration means that I embrace my life with love, joy, and serenity. I rejoice in others' accomplishments, and my own.

Celebration means to be fully present, knowing the "all-rightedness" and love in each moment. Celebration is to be at one with each and every moment, breathing it in, breathing it out. Being responsive with all that I am, and all that I have to give.

Celebration is an unconditional, euphoric participation in life.

Celebration, to me, is doing the work that passion generates, and that generates passion.

I'm continually lost in an effervescent fog, trying some new technical challenge, hoping to discover some marvelous combination to soothe my insatiable curiosity. To find that people respond to my work with, "Look, someone has said what I could not say; someone has made sense of this part of my life"—now *that's* living in celebration!

Celebration means to praise God every day for all the special talents, abilities, and potential He gave me.

Celebrating Your Dream

Celebration is a daily conversation with God—about all *the best* in His universe.

Feeling joyous, deserving of that joy, taking time to notice and mark accomplishments. It is thriving, not merely surviving.

Thornton Wilder in the play *Our Town* speaks through one of his characters: "Oh Earth, you are so wonderful. Do any human beings ever realize life while they live it, every minute?" To me, true celebration occurs when we are fully alive and celebrating each moment, each breath of life. My work in hospice has brought a profound change to my life. I am learning to let go and open myself more and more as I sit with those facing the ultimate surrender of letting go. I have lived a very rich life, full of intense joys and deep, painful sorrows. Now I see that all that has brought me to this place at this time. As Dag Hammarskjold pointed out, celebration can be summed up in the words: "For all that has been, thanks. For all that will be, yes!"

Giving Yourself Permission to Trust and Commit

By embracing the decision to face and triumph over any challenge, you unleash everything within you that cries out for expression. In other words, you are transformed! In one quantum leap, you find that the work you've committed yourself to do is no longer cumbersome. Instead, it is cause for rejoicing because in doing it you can more fully express the love, compassion, creativity, beauty, truth, and wisdom that is at the center of what you want to accomplish. And so you celebrate. Every day, you *consciously* appreciate that which carries you forward, that which makes the journey more fulfilling. Soon, celebration is a habit. You aren't there quite yet, you say. Instead, you are constantly called back to the world's reality because you must live from paycheck to paycheck—or because you remain in a "bad" relationship—or because you haven't yet found the "right" job! Well, if you are living for Fridays and vacations, take a closer look at what you are, and are not, doing to move forward.

> *Take a pen and write answers to:*
> ★ *What am I living* **from** *and* **to***?*
> ★ *Where would I rather be?*
> ★ *What would I rather be doing/having?*
> ★ *Do I* **want** *to live in the celebration of my highest dream? Why?*
> ★ *On a scale of 1 (struggling to survive) to 10 (expansive celebration), where do I place myself right now?*
> ★ *Am I living from choices, or reactions?*
> ★ *Am I living in my spirit energy?*
> ★ *Am I living in my personal power?*
> ★ *Am I living in joy?*
> ★ *What beginning action do I want to take to prepare for more celebration?*
> ★ *What regular action will I take to practice* **living** *in celebration?*

Let me tell you about some of the celebrations that followed having done the above. Many people gave themselves permission to get married, have children, start businesses, leave jobs, work through old hurts to heal their wounds, go back to college or acquire further training, volunteer for charitable work, and realign with their deepest dream selves. Each of them has stopped saying, "Someday, I'll. . . ." and are now setting aside time each day to celebrate *something*.

Celebrating at Work

I have found too few people who are including consistent celebration in their work-a-day world. It's perhaps they are surrounded by others who see joy in working as frivolous—as if those who are happy while working are not really serious about their jobs. As they see it, "serious" workers look forward to the *end* of the work day. Any rejoicing they do is reserved for *after* the work day is over. For many, celebrating is something to be waited for, like a party, a special night out, or a vacation. Certainly, it is not something they *do* every day, all day long. From their point of view, there must be a significant, socially acceptable reason to celebrate. Just as unfortunate, that type of person views celebration as something done to acknowledge what people do instead of what they are, limiting them to taking notice of measurable accomplishments made on the job, or the years spent doing it. But don't be limited by people who see celebration as coming from *outside* themselves—as an *external* reward. Remember, as you change, so do those around you. One of my clients did this very simply: each week she placed a piece of her valuable crystal collection on top of an office cabinet. Even in the muted light of florescent lighting, the crystal facets flung twinkles of light around the room. Amazingly, even this small physical change in the environment evoked attitudinal changes. So, change your attitude and start spreading your light.

Another example of on-the-job attitude is Rick, the bistro manager, who revels each day in meeting vacationers who regularly stop by for a meal, or a coffee latte. With them, he celebrates his memories of experiences he's had in their states or countries. Every day, he does this. Every hour—I told you that his was a successful bistro!

Celebrating in Times of Loss and Sorrow

How do you celebrate when you've just lost your job? When your latest attempt at realizing your dream has failed? Or when there has been a death or disaster in the family? You:

1] Acknowledge all of your feelings on and about the situation.
2] Acknowledge everyone else's feelings.
3] Allow yourself time to grieve and fear.
4] Allow others their grief and fears.
5] Meditate or pray to keep your connection with your inner spirit strong.

6] Step aside and re-evaluate where you are in your life.

7] Re-evaluate your dream—how will the loss affect it?

8] Know that you are still in charge of your dream.

9] Design a time frame in which you can move on through the pain and confusion to continue your life and dream.

10] Select the specific steps you will take to begin, follow through, and reach your dream.

These are the things that I did when we lost many of the physical things people ordinarily think of as necessary. But, you see, nothing about that has anything to do with me. It has nothing to do with celebrating, either. In times of difficulty, I look for things to celebrate. In fact, I look for things to celebrate all the time. Do you?

Knowing When and What to Celebrate

Remember a time when you went through the motions of celebrating and felt something was missing. What wasn't there? Or, was it that something was actually wrong? Family celebrations often fall into this category. While you are glad that cousin Amy found such a perfect husband, you'd also like one of your own. Added to your discomfort is the fact that everyone else is trying not to upset Aunt Marie by mentioning her recently deceased husband. Although she says nothing, when no one remarks upon how much he would have enjoyed the wedding, she is hurt. Around her, everyone keeps pretending that all is well. So, when the wedding reception is over, each *feels* an underlying sadness; a sense that something important has been left undone or unsaid. So everyone consoles him- or herself by getting back to "normal." But "normal" all too often means accepting or pretending that everything is alright. But not you.

Having come this far in your development, you know that feeling loss after a celebration is not normal. You also know that if you are not celebrating little things every day, you are still accepting the restrictive standards of those

Celebrating the Dream   **183**

around you. This is the time that dream activators go back and review their responses to the list of nots that tie them in knots. Recall the child you were before you accepted those restrictions. Enjoy once again the thrill and joy of being young and tasting all the new things the world offered. Be two again and inspect all the new stuff around you. Remember yourself at three, climbing anything and questioning everything. Do all those things again. And do them again, until you've moved beyond the restrictions that might still be holding you in bondage!

Celebrating Celebration

Now that you have come so far, take full measure of yourself. What do you as a powerful celebrant look like? How are you dressed when you are living and working your dream? What is your dream? How are those working around you attired? What do you think of them? What do they think of you? What do they say they like best about you? Which of their statements do you most appreciate? Whenever you are asked about your current dream, what is your reply? Do you suspect that it might one day be even higher?

What are the character traits you most value in yourself? Do you radiate your purpose to others? Outside of work, whom do you spend time with . . . and why? Which new outside activities do you enjoy? Why? Which activities do you commit yourself to because they support your dream, not because you enjoy them? What parts of your dream require money? Yours or someone else's? What else do you spend money on? Why? Are your daily habits and practices congruent with your dream? What activity do you want to be engaged in when you die?

Write an imaginary news magazine story describing you, and your full use of personal power in celebrating your ultimate dream. In this way, celebration becomes a lifestyle. Reread this often, always updating it as your world expands. And remember . . . Celebration is simply an attitude—a way of living every day of your life!

Thinking Personally, Acting Globally

We've all heard the expression "Think global, act local." I believe that it forces each of us to accept personal responsibility for saving the world when we turn that around to "Think local, act global." Every drop of water we squander, each aluminum can we throw way, and everything we consume eventually affects the rest of the world. The same is true of our dreams. By activating our own powers to make our dreams come true, we change our families, neighborhoods, cities, and nations. When enough of us are engaged in celebrating our fulfillment, we can revitalize life in every corner and byway of the planet. So, use your powers to fulfill your dream. Become even stronger by combining your power with that of other dream activators. And for those of you ready to work together to save our world, I invite you to share your dream scripts with others and join in the reformation of consciousness and accomplishment. And keep your one dream alive by celebrating everything in life every day.

Never Again...

Never again will you question whether or not to celebrate every step, every experience, every wish, hope, and dream realized. You are now choosing to live your *one* dream in the state of celebration.

Record your most jubilant life experiences that you have truly celebrated.

Celebrating Your Dream

Celebrating Your Dream

As a celebrated dream activator, you grow increasingly aware of every moment of each day. Become dedicated to enhancing your daily journey by recording some of your everyday celebrations.

Make the Dream Real... Make it Yours

Working toward a dream is at times fun and exhilarating despite challenges to your forward movement. Reaching a dream requires dedication, persistence, and acceptance of one's own power. It isn't easy, and aren't you glad that you are doing it?

List the biographical films or books that have shown you how to act in your moment of triumph.

Celebrating Your Dream

Describe the people who will be with you in spirit or body at the moment of your triumph.

Rejoice. You've created your own celebration. By doing that, you've made your dream a reality. You celebrate your life, those who support you, and your dream!

Contact Newcastle Publishing at (800) 932-4809 to order additional copies of the book. Quantity discounts are available to groups, organizations, and companies for any Newcastle title. All major credit cards accepted.

For more information on Joyce's workshops, books, consulting services, speaking engagements, and facilitating journaling groups, or if you simply want to share your story as an inspiring example of someone who is living his or her dream, write to:

Joyce Chapman
Live Your Dream
P.O. Box 283
Lincoln City, OR 97367